# dog breed guide for kids

## 50 Essential Dog Breeds to Know and Love with Fun Facts and Tips for Care

Christine Rohloff Gossinger

ROCKRIDGE
PRESS

For general information on our other products and services or to obtain technical support, please contact our Customer Care Department within the United States at (866) 744-2665, or outside the United States at (510) 253-0500.

Rockridge Press publishes its books in a variety of electronic and print formats. Some content that appears in print may not be available in electronic books, and vice versa.

Interior and Cover Designer: Sean Doyle/Chiaka John
Art Producer: Alyssa Williams
Editor: Elizabeth Baird
Production Editor: Ellina Litmanovich
Production Manager: Martin Worthington

Copyright Page: All images used under license from Shutterstock and iStock.

Author photo courtesy Mykell Gossinger

Paperback ISBN: 978-1-63807-083-2
eBook ISBN: 978-1-63807-830-2
R0

To my husband, Mykell, for his inspiring
humor and unwavering support, and
to my fur babies, Rudy and Bobby, for
countless life lessons and connecting me
to my true life's purpose.

# Contents

# Introduction

One of my first childhood memories is sitting on a sleigh as our St. Bernard, Heidi, pulled me through the snow. She was my loyal protector and my first "best friend." I have been blessed with many furry best friends over the years. I believe that each dog came to me to teach me whatever lesson I needed to learn in that moment. Some taught me patience, others forgiveness and acceptance. All taught me the beauty of living in the moment and loving unconditionally. My cocker spaniels, Rudy and Bobby, even connected me to my life's purpose—becoming a dog trainer.

In my experience as a dog trainer, the number-one piece of the canine puzzle often overlooked is the breed of the dog. As trainers we are asked to "fix" what are seen as problem behaviors when what we need to consider is the breed's original purpose and how we can have the dog express these "instincts" in a way that works for both dog and human. No breeds are "good" or "bad"; they are just different (very much like us humans!). We all thrive in different environments.

This book is designed to give you an overview of some of the world's most popular and iconic breeds so that you may better understand what their needs are and what is involved in caring for them. Whether you are looking for your next "fur-ever" friend, are curious about different breeds, or simply just love dogs like I do, I hope this will be a valuable resource.

The breeds in this book are organized according to the seven American Kennel Club (AKC) breed groups and represent a wide variety of dogs. You can read about one group at a time, go straight to your favorites, or bounce around wherever your interests lead you.

# WHAT IS A DOG BREED?

The dog you choose to bring into your family will be your companion for many years to come, so it is very important that you and your dog are a good match. Every breed has its own personality, as well as its own exercise, training, and grooming needs.

A dog breed is the label for a group of dogs that, through careful breeding by humans, has evolved to have certain traits or perform certain tasks, like hunting, guarding, or herding. Dogs of the same breed share a common ancestor and have similar looks and personalities. For example, French bulldogs have big pointy ears and short, stocky bodies that make them easily recognizable as Frenchies.

As humans thought of new jobs for dogs to do and discovered better breeding practices, they created more and more breeds with very distinct qualities. Over the last 200 years, the number of dog breeds has gone from a handful to hundreds. Each breed has an ideal set of physical traits and talents. This is called a breed standard.

Breed clubs record the breed standard in a written document that is approved by the American Kennel Club (AKC). Although there are somewhere between 350 and 450 breeds worldwide, the AKC currently only officially recognizes 197 breeds. The AKC places these breeds into one of seven groups based on a particular set of jobs they perform or qualities they possess. They are:

## Sporting Group

Sporting dogs, also called gun dogs or bird dogs, were bred to work closely with hunters to find, flush (chase), and retrieve birds. This group includes retrievers, setters, spaniels, and pointers. Because they were bred to work closely with humans, they are highly trainable and make loving companions, as well as wonderful service and therapy dogs.

## Hound Group

Originally bred for hunting, the hound group is divided into scent hounds and sight hounds. Scent hounds have powerful noses and long ears to detect and track what they are looking for. Sight hounds have sharp vision and sleek, long-legged bodies to find and catch game. They are known for their incredible speed. Both scent and sight hounds are intelligent, curious, very vocal, and independent.

## Working Group

Most of the ancient breeds fall into this group, which were first bred to help humans with practical duties, such as protection for people or livestock and pulling carts or sleds. They are loyal, strong, and smart.

## Terrier Group

This group was initially bred to hunt small animals, like foxes and rats. Known to be strong-willed, feisty, and fun, with energy to burn, they come in all shapes and sizes. The shorter-legged terriers, like the Jack Russell, were bred to burrow underground in pursuit of rodents, while those of the longer-legged variety, like the bull terrier, were bred to dig out vermin. All terriers can be fierce watchdogs as well as beloved family pets.

## Toy Group

Dogs in this group, like the Chihuahua and Pomeranian, are small in size but big in personality. They were bred specifically

to be companions or lapdogs and make loving, affectionate family members.

## Nonsporting Group

This is a catchall group for breeds that do not fit into any of the other groups. It includes dogs whose jobs are outdated so they are now companion dogs and dogs whose original role was that of a specialty pet for nobility and royalty. This group has all sizes, shapes, and personalities.

## Herding Group

Bred to herd livestock like goats, sheep, and even reindeer, these dogs are extremely smart with boundless energy. Since they were bred to work closely with their handler, they are highly trainable and are happiest when with their family. They need lots of physical and mental exercise and are at their best when they have a job to do.

# FROM WOLF TO FURRY FRIEND

All dogs share a common ancestor, the gray wolf. Although this ancient relative is obvious in some breeds, like the Siberian husky, it is not as apparent in others, like the poodle, Chihuahua, or beagle. However, if you look beyond the outward appearance and into the DNA of any dog, you will be amazed to find that it is practically identical to that of a wolf.

The transition from wild animal to domesticated companion began with random changes in wolves' size and shape, but it picked up speed when humans began carefully breeding dogs that had the qualities they desired.

This split between wolf and dog is thought to have begun between 15,000 and 40,000 years ago. Some theories suggest our early ancestors took in wolf cubs as pets, cave guardians, and hunting companions. But other scholars believe that wolves became used to living around humans and somehow domesticated themselves. Regardless of how exactly it happened, we know that today's breeds can be traced back thousands of years to this beautiful wild ancestor.

# DIFFERENT SHADES OF DOG LOVE

There are three categories of dog to consider: purebred, crossbred, or mixed breed.

When you hear the words "dog breed," the first thing most people think of is purebred dogs. A purebred puppy is the offspring of two dogs of the same breed that conform to the AKC breed standard. Purebred dogs will look similar and will also share common personality and behavior traits.

A crossbred puppy is the offspring of two different purebred dogs. The breeding is intentional, with the goal of combining the best qualities of both breeds. This breeding began in the 1950s, but it really exploded in the last 10 years with the "doodle" phenomenon (dogs like golden doodles, Labradoodles, and Bernedoodles). All "doodles" are breeds that have been crossed with poodles since poodles don't shed and are hypoallergenic (unlikely to cause an allergic reaction).

Mixed breeds comprise the rest of the dog population. They have two or more breeds in their DNA. These dogs have usually inherited a blend of physical and personality traits. Often, it is difficult to know exactly what breeds are in their makeup.

Purebreds, crossbreds, and mixed breeds all bring with them their own set of strengths and challenges. One is not necessarily better than another. What is important is that the dog and family are a good fit.

# A DOG'S JOURNEY HOME

The best way to ensure that you and a dog are a match made in heaven is to seek the help of a responsible and experienced breeder, shelter, or rescue organization.

Opinions on which resource to use are as varied as the number of breeds. Most people have very strong feelings on the subject. Do your homework to make sure that whomever you choose is knowledgeable and has the best interests of the dog and you in mind.

Good breeders will allow you to visit and see where their puppies spend the first 8 to 10 weeks of their lives. They test the health of their puppies, adhere to the AKC breed standard, and take the time to socialize their puppies. Breeders deal exclusively with purebreds and crossbreds for purchase.

Shelters, whether public or private, primarily have mixed breeds for adoption. There you will find everything from young puppies to older dogs in need of new homes. Shelters have a facility or central location to house their dogs.

Rescues also have primarily mixed breeds, although there are also breed-specific rescues for those who have their hearts set on a particular breed. These rescues do not work out of a specific location, but usually rely on foster families who care for these dogs in their homes until they are adopted.

# DOG ADOPTION AND FOSTERING

Shelters and rescues are filled with happy, healthy dogs waiting to find their forever families. There are many benefits to adopting a rescue dog to be your furry companion. Often these dogs are past the puppy phase and are already housebroken. Adopting a dog also makes room for another homeless animal in the shelter. Most of all, you will change a dog's life for the better while getting a new best friend.

Both shelters and rescues often use social media or online platforms to get the word out about their dogs up for adoption. PetFinder.com is one of the best-known searchable online databases of animals looking for their forever homes, in addition to being a directory of nearly 11,000 animal shelters and rescues across the United States, Canada, and Mexico.

The following websites are also great resources:

PetsmartCharities.com

BestFriends.org

TheShelterProject.com

AKC.org/akc-rescue-network

For those who may not be ready to adopt, rescues and shelters are always looking for people to foster dogs. Fostering involves housing and caring for a dog for a certain amount of time or until the dog finds a forever home. Fostering can also be a wonderful chance to see if the dog is a good fit for you before considering adoption.

# COMMON DOG QUESTIONS

**Q: Do dogs see only in black and white?**

A: No. Dogs see several colors, specifically blue, yellow, and gray. Their color spectrum is just less vivid than ours.

**Q: What is the smallest dog breed? What is the largest dog breed?**

A: The smallest breed of dog is the Chihuahua, standing at a mere 6 to 9 inches tall and weighing from 2 to 6 pounds. The tallest is the Irish wolfhound, standing at 34 inches tall. The heaviest is the English mastiff, averaging 200 to 230 pounds!

**Q: How much better is a dog's hearing compared to ours?**

A: Dogs can hear four times better than humans. They also have two times the number of muscles in their ears as humans. This enables them to move their ears independently.

**Q: How many times greater is a dog's sense of smell compared to ours? Which breed has the best sense of smell?**

A: A dog's sense of smell is 10,000 times greater than ours. This is because they have 300 million olfactory (smell) receptors, compared to our 6 million. Also, it is interesting to note that a dog's nose print is unique, just like a human's fingerprint. Each dog's nose has its own pattern of ridges and creases. The bloodhound is the breed with the strongest sense of smell.

**Q: How many words can the average dog learn?**

A: When it comes to language, the average dog can learn about 165 words. However, "superdogs" (those in the top 20 percent of dog intelligence) can learn about 250. The "superdog" estimate is based on a study of a border collie named Rico who showed knowledge of over 200 words.

**Q: What dog breed is the fastest?**

A: Clocking in at more than 40 miles per hour, greyhounds are the fastest breed. They could even beat a cheetah in a race. Cheetahs may be able to run twice as fast, but they can only maintain that top speed for 30 seconds, while greyhounds can maintain a speed of 35 to 40 miles per hour for up to seven miles.

**Q: What breed of dog has the longest ears?**

A: Basset hounds have the longest ears. In fact, one basset hound named Jack is in the *Guinness Book of World Records* for having the longest ears, at 17 inches long. Basset hounds also have a sense of smell second only to the bloodhound, but it is not just the nose doing the work. Their long ears help stir smells upward toward the nose.

**Q: What breed(s) of dogs are most commonly used as service dogs?**

A: The most common breeds that come to mind when you think of service dogs are the Labrador retriever, golden retriever, and German shepherd. However, breeds like the poodle, Great Dane, and even the American Staffordshire terrier have been known to be exceptional for a wide variety of service dog tasks.

**Q: Which dog breeds are best for people with allergies?**

A: The Yorkshire terrier's long silky hair is almost identical to human hair, which makes the breed a good choice for those with pet allergies. Other breeds suggested for people with allergies are the poodle, Havanese, miniature schnauzer, Bedlington terrier, and Lagotto Romagnolo.

**Q: Which breed is the most popular?**

A: The most popular breeds are always changing, but according to the most recent AKC data, the Labrador retriever once again ranked as the number-one most popular breed in the United States. This breed has been in the top 10 for 30 consecutive years, longer than any other breed. The rest of the breeds currently rounding out the top 10 are: French bulldogs, German shepherds, golden retrievers, bulldogs, poodles, beagles, rottweilers, German shorthaired pointers, and dachshunds.

**Q: Has a dog ever won an Academy Award?**

A: At the first Academy Awards, a German shepherd named Rin Tin Tin supposedly received the most votes for Best Actor. However, the Academy wanted to be taken seriously, so they held another vote after taking this canine movie star off the ballot.

**Q: What is the oldest known dog breed?**

A: The world's oldest known breed of domesticated dog is the saluki. This breed is believed to have first emerged in 329 BCE and was admired in ancient Egypt as a royal pet.

**Q: Do dogs dream?**

A: All dogs dream. When it comes to how frequently, it depends on the dog's size. Smaller dogs, like the Chihuahua, tend to dream more often during the night than large dogs do. Puppies also experience more dreams than adult dogs since they acquire huge amounts of new information daily and have more to process at night.

# DOG SAFETY

Dogs add so much joy to our lives, but no matter how easygoing, friendly, and patient a dog may be, any dog can become frightened or uncomfortable in certain situations. They cannot tell us in words how they are feeling, so they can sometimes react in a way that may threaten our safety and theirs.

Here are a few safety tips for protecting the welfare of both dog and human:

1. Always ask a dog's owner(s) if it is okay to approach and pet their dog.

2. Even with the owner's permission, first observe the dog's body language. If the dog's body becomes stiff, their tail is tucked, or their ears are back, do not approach or attempt to touch the dog.

3. Always be aware of your own body language. Approach slowly and calmly without making direct eye contact and always give dogs their space.

4. Do not reach over a dog's head to pet them. Instead, pet their chest.

5. Never put your face by the dog's face, especially if it is a dog you do not know.

6. Do not touch a dog that is sleeping or eating.

7. Never try to remove anything from a dog's mouth.

**CHAPTER 1**

# SPORTING GROUP

**Sporting dogs, which include** retrievers, spaniels, setters, and pointers, were originally bred to assist hunters with finding and retrieving birds. Known for their remarkable instincts in the water and woods, many bird dogs still are active in the field with hunters today. They are alert, athletic, confident, good-natured, and highly trainable. These qualities also make them outstanding therapy, assistance, and search and rescue dogs, as well as loyal companions and family members. Their spirited personalities, intelligence, and high energy make both physical and mental exercise a must. They thrive in activities like swimming, flyball, and agility, a sport where dogs race through obstacle courses. Many sporting dogs, including the Labrador retriever and golden retriever, consistently make the top 10 list of most popular breeds every year.

# COCKER SPANIEL

## PHYSICAL CHARACTERISTICS

This beautiful breed can be identified by their round, dark eyes, long, soft ears, and docked tails.* They are medium size in stature, standing about 14 or 15 inches tall, and weighing about 25 to 30 pounds.

Cockers come in a variety of shades that are separated into three groups: black, ASCOB (any solid color other than black), and parti-color (white with patches of another color, like black).

## PERSONALITY

The cocker's nickname, Merry Cocker, comes from their cheerful personality. These sporty spaniels want nothing more than to be included in family activities, whether that is romping in the yard, taking a long walk, or snuggling on the couch. Their intelligence, desire to work for treats, and strong need to make their people happy make them highly trainable.

## HISTORY

The cocker spaniel was originally bred in England as a hunting and bird dog. In fact, the name "cocker" comes from the bird it was trained to hunt, the woodcock.

The breed, then known as the English cocker, was brought to America in the early 1600s. American breeders began to make physical changes to the breed, and in the early 1940s, the American cocker was recognized as a separate breed from the English cocker. Since then, the American cocker has become one of the most beloved breeds in the country, holding the record for most years at the top of the most popular breeds list.

### Caretaking Tips

Cocker spaniels are known for their long, feathery ears and silky coat, making regular grooming a must. Daily brushing, weekly ear cleanings, and regular bathing with shampoo that is gentle on their sensitive skin are very important for the cocker's health and well-being. Monthly professional grooming is often needed.

Cockers need some form of daily exercise to keep physically fit and stay at a healthy weight. Mental exercise is also important. They love nothing more than learning new tricks.

*Docking a puppy's tail means to remove a portion of it, usually when the pup is only a few days old. Some sporting and working dogs traditionally have their tails docked to decrease injury risk when hunting, herding, or working in the field.*

# GERMAN SHORTHAIRED POINTER

## PHYSICAL APPEARANCE

This bird dog has a sleek, muscular build, a short, thick coat, docked tail, and webbed feet that make it an effective hunting companion both on land and in water. The silhouette of a German shorthaired pointer "locked on point," when it stands motionless with its nose pointing toward an object and one paw raised, is a sight to behold. It has led to its appearance being described as both noble and aristocratic.

Their medium stature ranges from 21 to 25 inches tall and 45 to 70 pounds. Their durable coat comes in a solid liver color (reddish brown) or most commonly in distinctive patterns of liver and white. It also comes in black, black and white, and roan (white mixed with other colors).

## PERSONALITY

The German shorthaired pointer, or GSP, is celebrated for its power, speed, and endurance. However, it is the GSP's friendly disposition, intelligence, and highly trainable nature that make these dogs beloved best friends, albeit not always easy ones due to their high energy and exercise needs. Yet, if you can fulfill those needs, they are known to bond strongly with their family.

**DID YOU KNOW?**

- Although GSPs were primarily bred to hunt, they have also been used to guard homes, pull sleds, and sniff for bombs.

- Unlike other breeds, the color of their nose always matches the color of their coat.

## HISTORY

The origins of the German shorthaired pointer date back to the 1800s when German breeders wanted to create the ultimate hunting dog. To date, GSPs are one of the most accomplished all-around hunting and sporting breeds. Although many are still used for hunting today, it is more likely that most have become cherished family members.

### Caretaking Tips

An active lifestyle is essential for focusing the GSP's rambunctious nature into a positive outlet. They are an extremely high-energy breed with incredible stamina and thrive on vigorous exercise twice a day. Thankfully, their grooming needs are far less time-consuming. A quick once-over with a brush a few times a month is sufficient.

# GOLDEN RETRIEVER

## PHYSICAL CHARACTERISTICS

This joyful breed is best known for its gorgeous, golden, feathery coat and big brown eyes. These dogs are natural athletes, possessing a muscular medium to large build. They usually stand between 22 and 24 inches tall and weigh between 55 and 75 pounds.

## PERSONALITY

Their playfulness, natural patience, and unmatched devotion to their family make them the most loyal of companions. They are also extremely intelligent. Their high IQ and overall eagerness to please their people make them highly trainable. It is no surprise that they consistently rank in the top three most popular breeds in the United States every year.

## HISTORY

The golden retriever was originally a Scottish gun dog that was bred to retrieve waterfowl like ducks and upland game birds. Lord Tweedmouth, who lived in the Scottish Highlands, first developed the breed in the mid to late 1800s. Today, the versatile golden retriever's jobs include hunting and tracking, search and rescue, therapy, service, or guide dog, as well as beloved companion and family member.

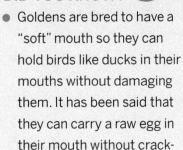

## DID YOU KNOW?

- Goldens are bred to have a "soft" mouth so they can hold birds like ducks in their mouths without damaging them. It has been said that they can carry a raw egg in their mouth without cracking the shell.

- Golden retrievers come in three colors: golden, light golden, and dark golden. They also come in three different breed types: English, Canadian, and American.

## Caretaking Tips

Golden retrievers need lots of physical and mental exercise to keep them healthy, happy, and out of trouble. Since they love nothing more than being with their family, it is important to find activities that you can do together like obedience training or rally (in which a dog follows a set course). Most golden retrievers love the water, so swimming is also a good way to meet their exercise needs.

The golden retriever's thick, water-repellent double coat (consisting of two layers) sheds heavily twice a year and moderately throughout the rest of the year, making daily brushing and a monthly visit to the groomer necessary.

# IRISH SETTER

## PHYSICAL APPEARANCE

The Irish setter stands out with its flashy, silky red coat, long legs and neck, and elegant yet substantial build. Because of its beautiful red coat, it is called *Modder Rhu,* meaning "red dog" in Gaelic. However, do not let this breed's gorgeous appearance fool you. They are as bold and rugged as they are beautiful and graceful. They stand about 27 inches tall and weigh about 70 pounds.

## PERSONALITY

Irish setters are rambunctious redheads that remain puppies at heart for most of their lives. Their sweet, sensitive, and happy-go-lucky nature makes them loveable family members. Their high level of intelligence makes it important for them to be given appropriate jobs or tasks to focus on so they do not become bored and give in to their fondness for mischief. However, it is also this clownish attitude that can make them such fun companions.

## HISTORY

Irish hunters of the 1800s bred "red setters" by combining the best traits from several breeds, including the English setter, pointer, Irish terrier, and Irish water spaniel. What developed from these breeds was a superb bird dog with a strong hunting instinct and a sharp

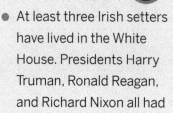

**DID YOU KNOW?**

- At least three Irish setters have lived in the White House. Presidents Harry Truman, Ronald Reagan, and Richard Nixon all had Irish setters.

- Although the most distinguishing feature is their flashy red coat, Irish setters were originally bred to be red and white so hunters could better spot them in the field.

nose. Although this setter was bred to "set," or crouch, next to prey, they can also hold a pointing position. The breed was brought to the United States in the 19th century.

Today, the Irish setter is found less often in the field and more often in family homes. They also make wonderful therapy and assistance dogs.

## Caretaking Tips

Surprisingly, the Irish setter's famous red coat only requires moderate grooming. Brushing their coat twice weekly is sufficient.

However, their exercise and training needs are much more extensive. Like other hunting breeds, the Irish setter is highly energetic and requires plenty of daily exercise and mental stimulation. Daily walks, vigorous play sessions, and canine sports are all wonderful ways to satisfy these needs.

# LABRADOR RETRIEVER

### PHYSICAL APPEARANCE

Labrador retrievers, or Labs, are notable for their broad head, drop ears, and large, soulful eyes. Their medium to large build ranges from 21.5 to 24.5 inches tall and 55 to 80 pounds.

Two of their most pronounced features are the thick, but fairly short, water-repellent double coat that comes in black, yellow, and chocolate, and their well-known "otter tail." A Lab's tail acts like a rudder, moving back and forth to aid them in turning when they swim.

### PERSONALITY

The outgoing, good-natured, and enthusiastic temperament of the Lab has made this breed an iconic family favorite for decades. Their easygoing attitude allows them to get along well

with people, dogs, and other pets, and their willingness to please makes them highly trainable.

Keep in mind, however, that this high-spirited breed has great energy and stamina. Sufficient exercise and training are essential to bring out their best qualities.

## HISTORY

Due to its popularity in the United States, it is easy to think of the Labrador retriever as an American breed. However, Labs' roots go back to Canada, not the US. They were first bred in Newfoundland, where

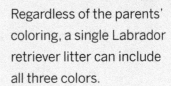

**DID YOU KNOW?**
Regardless of the parents' coloring, a single Labrador retriever litter can include all three colors.

they were traditional water dogs employed to work alongside fishermen to retrieve ducks. Around the 1800s, hunters and farmers in the US learned of the breed's work ethic and began incorporating Labs into their daily lives.

Through the years, Labs continued to work as hunting companions. However, today they serve in many diverse roles, including search and rescue, service, therapy dogs, and, above all, cherished companions.

## Caretaking Tips

Labrador retrievers are an intelligent, highly active breed that requires lots of daily physical exercise as well as plenty of mental stimulation. Daily physical activities will also help them maintain a healthy weight, as the breed is often predisposed to weight gain.

Despite a great deal of shedding, grooming needs for this breed are more on the moderate side. Brushing two to four times weekly is enough to keep their coat healthy.

# LAGOTTO ROMAGNOLO

**PHYSICAL APPEARANCE**

The Lagotto Romagnolo is small to medium in size with a muscular build. They average 14 to 19 inches in height and weigh 28 to 35 pounds.

Their wooly textured coat with tight, ring-shaped curls comes in a variety of colors, including off-white, white with brown, or orange patches and brown roan. These wooly curls cover their entire body and are offset by a lavish beard,

**DID YOU KNOW?**

The AKC only recently accepted Lagotto Romagnolos into the Sporting Group in 2015. However, the breed is actually very old and is believed to be the ancestor of all water dogs (breeds like the Portuguese water dog and the American water spaniel). Ancient artifacts dating back to anywhere between the 8th and 2nd century BCE depict hunting dogs that look very much like the Lagotto Romagnolo.

eyebrows, and whiskers. These curls feel and behave more like hair than fur, which means they don't shed very much and are great options for those allergic to dogs.

## PERSONALITY

These dogs are highly intelligent, alert, lively, and eager to learn. They can make affectionate companions who bond closely to their families, as well as good watchdogs who are very sensitive to their environment. The qualities they develop depend on breeding, socialization, and early training.

## HISTORY

This Italian breed goes as far back as the Italian Renaissance when it was originally bred as a waterfowl retriever. However, early breeders found that their exceptional nose was best used in the countryside rooting out truffles, an Italian delicacy like a mushroom. They are considered the world's finest truffle hunting dog, hence their nickname Truffle.

### Caretaking Tips

This breed doesn't need as much vigorous exercise as their sporting group counterparts, but they still need to have an active and engaged life to be truly happy.

Swimming and nose work are wonderful outlets since they love water and have an extremely sharp sense of smell. They are very bonded to their people and love being a part of family activities. They tend to be wary of strangers, so early socialization and training is essential.

Even though they do not shed, they need regular grooming to keep their plush coat healthy and tangle free.

# VIZSLA

**PHYSICAL APPEARANCE**

The vizsla is a lean, muscular dog of medium stature. They are usually 21 to 24 inches tall and weigh between 45 and 60 pounds.

The breed's sleek, athletic body has a golden red coat that is short and smooth and blends perfectly with their big brown eyes. This even brown tone makes them great at camouflaging, which is helpful when hunting.

**PERSONALITY**

This rugged yet elegant breed is known for its high energy, intense focus, and stamina in the field as well as its gentle, highly affectionate, and sensitive nature at home.

Intelligent and deeply curious, vizslas work hard and play even harder. However, at the end of the day, they want nothing more than to snuggle with their family. In fact, many say that getting a vizsla is a little like getting another shadow. Vizslas bond strongly with their families and do not enjoy being left alone, earning them the nickname Velcro Dog.

## HISTORY

Scholars believe this Hungarian gun dog may have originated in the 9th century. According to the AKC, the Magyar people, who left Russia and came to Hungary in the mid-800s, bred the ancestors of the vizsla. The Magyar cavalry was known for their speed, agility, and toughness and bred these qualities into their dogs.

### Caretaking Tips

A vizsla is both a star athlete and straight-A student, so lots of daily physical and mental exercise is needed. Agility games and long walks are good, but the chance to run hard and fast is even better. They make for great jogging companions once they are mature. In fact, at top speed, vizslas can reach 40 miles per hour and are one of the top 10 fastest dog breeds. Vizslas do not enjoy being apart from their family, so early training to build their comfort level being left alone is a must.

Grooming needs are basic since they have fine short hair with no insulating undercoat.

# CHAPTER 2

# HOUND GROUP

**The hound group consists** of hunting dogs that were bred and trained to track animals by sight or scent. Sight hounds, like greyhounds, use their sharp eyes to find game and use their agility and speed to chase it. They have lean bodies, deep chests, and long legs. Scent hounds, like the bloodhound, use their powerful noses to track game and use their incredible endurance to find it. They tend to be shorter in stature with long ears that help stir up scents from the ground. Although hounds are a diverse group in physical appearance and behavior, they share an independent nature, a high intelligence, a healthy curiosity, and the distinct ability to bay—a unique howl that you will never forget once you hear it. This ability was bred into many hounds so that hunters could find them when they were far away tracking game.

# BASENJI

### PHYSICAL CHARACTERISTICS

Basenjis have finely chiseled features, pricked ears, and beautifully expressive almond eyes. They have a short red coat and a tail that tightly curls over their back. They are small and graceful, reaching around 17 inches in height and weighing about 24 pounds.

### PERSONALITY

Basenjis are a breed of great intelligence, poise, and independence. They are also highly curious canines with a fondness for mischief. Many fans of the breed describe them as catlike. They are famous for their keen eyesight and excellent sense of smell.

Although they can be shy with strangers, they are extremely affectionate, fun loving, and deeply devoted to and protective of their family.

### HISTORY

Basenjis are one of the oldest dog breeds. Cave paintings from as early as 6000 BCE show hunters with Basenji-like dogs that have curled tails and pricked ears. These dogs are also depicted on ancient Egyptian artifacts.

They survived thousands of years in Central Africa because of their bravery and ability to hunt big game. In Kenya, they were used to lure lions out of caves.

**DID YOU KNOW?**

- Many Basenjis are afraid of the dark. Their ancestors were bred to fear the dark because there was greater danger due to nighttime predators.

- The Basenji is known as the barkless dog because they make an unusual yodel-like sound instead of a bark.

In the late 1930s, they were brought to the United States. Although they remain skilled hunters, they have gained greater popularity as family companions.

## Caretaking Tips

Basenjis do best with an active lifestyle that provides both physical and mental exercise. One important thing to remember is that all exercise activities should be on a leash or in a secured yard. They should never be allowed to run loose since their strong hunting instincts may lead them to run off.

Basenjis groom themselves like cats and are known for their exceptionally clean coats. They only require occasional brushing and rarely need bathing.

# BASSET HOUND

## PHYSICAL CHARACTERISTICS

Basset hounds are one of the most recognizable breeds with their long, low body, floppy ears, short legs, droopy skin, and soft, sad-looking eyes. Their coat is short and smooth and comes in a variety of colors, tricolor being the most common.

They are short in stature but medium in build. Males are around 14 inches tall and 50 to 60 pounds, and females are 13 inches tall and 40 to 55 pounds. Despite their smaller size, they are big in strength and stamina. Their powerful legs and massive paws can take them over all types of terrain for long stretches of time.

## PERSONALITY

Basset hounds are smart, powerful, and determined in the field, making them exceptional hunting dogs. They are equally affectionate, gentle, patient, loyal, and silly at home. Their low-key charm and clownish nature bring endless smiles and laughter to their families. This scent hound is second only to the bloodhound when it comes to their powerful sense of smell.

## HISTORY

The basset hound is descended from dogs bred by French monks. By the 1500s, French hunters were using basset hounds to track small game like rabbits. They were excellent trackers and favored by hunters who liked that they could keep up with their slower stride.

They were exported to England and the United States in the late 1800s. Once in the United States, their main role changed from hunting dog to family companion.

### Caretaking Tips

Unlike other hounds, basset hounds only require moderate exercise. Daily walks at an average pace and short play sessions are usually enough to satisfy their exercise needs.

Grooming needs are also moderate. Weekly brushing, monthly bathing, and regular inspections of their eyes and ears will keep this breed happy and healthy.

# BEAGLE

## PHYSICAL CHARACTERISTICS

Beagles are solid, compact scent hounds with floppy ears, a perky tail, and an adorable face with large, expressive eyes. They range from 13 to 15 inches in height and weigh 18 to 30 pounds.

The breed's short, dense coat is usually tricolor (having three different colors), but it can also be lemon and white or red and white. They have tan markings on their face, a white blaze on their head, and a white tip on their tail. This white tip is also known as a flag because it was how hunters could spot them in the field.

## PERSONALITY

Beagles are active, clever, funny, and cheerful. They are also incredibly patient and great with children. All these qualities have

made them one of the most popular hound breeds for families over the years.

## HISTORY

This breed was likely developed from other English scent hounds, like the harrier. At the beginning of the 16th century, packs of beagle type hounds were used to hunt hare and rabbit.

In 1885, the AKC first recognized the beagle as a breed. The breed's popularity, first as a hunting dog and now as a companion, remains strong.

Beagles are also used by law enforcement to sniff out explosives, illegal substances, and pests. The Beagle Brigade keeps everyone safe patrolling baggage claims at more than 20 international airports.

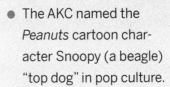

**DID YOU KNOW?**

- The AKC named the *Peanuts* cartoon character Snoopy (a beagle) "top dog" in pop culture.

- Beagles are one of the most vocal dog breeds. They can make three different sounds: a standard bark, a yodel-like sound called a bay, and a howl.

### Caretaking Tips

Beagles do best with an active lifestyle that involves at least one hour of daily exercise. Opportunities to run are ideal, but like all hounds, they need to exercise in a secured yard so they can't run off while tracking a scent.

They are highly sociable and do not do well when left alone for long periods of time. Early reward-based training (treats) and activities like nose work keep them happy and out of trouble.

Weekly brushing is sufficient to maintain a healthy coat.

# BLOODHOUND

### PHYSICAL CHARACTERISTICS

The bloodhound is famous for its long, wrinkled face, droopy ears, deep-set eyes, and solemn expression. They are rugged and powerful dogs with a massive build. They range in height from 23 to 27 inches and weigh between 80 and 110 pounds. Their short, dense coat is weatherproof and comes in red, liver and tan, or black and tan.

### PERSONALITY

Bloodhounds are the ultimate scent hound, often referred to as "a nose with a dog attached." They can track a scent up to 12 days after the source has left the area! They also have a very distinct bark and tend to be very vocal.

At home, the bloodhound is a loving, gentle, mild-mannered companion that brings endless joy to the family.

### HISTORY

Bloodhounds were first developed in a Belgian monastery around 1000 CE. In 1066, William the Conqueror brought this breed to England, where it captured the interest of Queen Victoria. The nobility began keeping records of the breed's bloodlines, which is where the bloodhound got its name. Prior to the bloodhound, there had been few records kept on dogs' bloodlines. Originally bred to hunt deer and wild boar, today their incredible noses are responsible for tracking everything from foxes and wolves to beloved lost pets and missing people.

**DID YOU KNOW?**
Their sense of smell is so powerful that the results of their nose work are considered admissible evidence in a court of law.

## Caretaking Tips

Bloodhounds are active dogs requiring daily exercise. Long daily walks or any chance to run are ideal outlets for them. They must be on a leash or in a secured area since their powerful sense of smell will lead them to wander. Nose work classes are also helpful for satisfying their powerful need to sniff. Bloodhounds are independent and can become set in their ways, so early obedience training will be necessary.

Grooming needs are moderate and involve regular bathing, ear cleaning, and weekly brushing. They are known to drool, so you will need to keep lots of towels around the house.

# DACHSHUND

### PHYSICAL CHARACTERISTICS

The dachshund's short stature, long body, floppy ears, and ever-alert expression make these dogs easily identifiable and adorable.

Dachshunds come in two sizes: miniature (5 to 6 inches tall and 11 pounds or under) and standard (8 to 9 inches tall and 16 to 32 pounds). They also come in three varieties: smooth, longhaired, or wirehaired. They come in a wide variety of colors.

### PERSONALITY

The dachshund is a small dog with a big personality. Their "big-dog" bark and spunky, brave, and protective side make them excellent watchdogs. Even though they're quite intelligent

and pick up skills easily, they are known to be one of the harder breeds to train due to their stubborn and independent nature. However, they have an equally soft and loving side that makes them popular family companions.

## HISTORY

Dachshunds date back to about the 16th century, when they were specifically bred to hunt badgers. In fact, "dachshund" translates to "badger dog" in German. Their short legs and determined nature were perfect for digging into tunnels and fighting badgers.

The breed was recognized by the AKC in 1885. They grew in popularity in the US in the 1950s and have remained a sought-after companion dog ever since.

### Caretaking Tips

Grooming needs depend on the type of coat. The longhaired variety requires daily brushing but not usually professional grooming. The wirehaired variety may need professional grooming but not necessarily daily brushing. Smooth-coated dachshunds shed more than the other varieties, but overall they have more moderate grooming needs.

They need plenty of physical exercise. Two walks of moderate length will help build their muscles and support their back. They are also highly intelligent, so mental stimulation in the form of obedience training and nose work will go a long way. Patience, consistency, and creativity are essential in training your independent and strong-willed dachshund.

# GREYHOUND

## PHYSICAL CHARACTERISTICS

The greyhound is built for speed, with its narrow head, long neck, muscular hind-quarters, and shock-absorbing paw pads. They can run over 40 miles per hour for up to seven miles! Their powerful bodies range in size from 27 to 30 inches tall and 55 to 88 pounds. Their short, smooth coat comes in many colors.

## PERSONALITY

Greyhounds are sweet-tempered, patient, and relatively quiet. Although some-what reserved with strangers,

they are affectionate and cuddly with their family members. They won't hesitate to climb in laps, despite their larger-than-lapdog size!

## HISTORY

Greyhounds are one of the world's oldest breeds, dating back to ancient Egypt. In that time, they were honored as gods and could only be owned by royalty.

Until the 20th century, greyhounds were bred for hunting small game. In the 1920s, greyhound racing was introduced as a competitive sport in which greyhounds race around a track in pursuit of a lure, often meant to resemble a rabbit. Today, due to the concern that the sport is a danger to the dogs' health, there is a movement to move away from racing and find homes for retired racing dogs. Greyhound rescues have made real progress, and now the greyhound's primary role is as a loving family companion.

## Caretaking Tips

Despite their incredible speed, greyhounds only require moderate exercise. They are just as happy lounging at home as running around. Greyhounds also have a very high prey drive (the instinct to chase and capture prey), so when off leash, they must be in a secured area to keep them from running off.

Their short coat needs little in the way of daily care. However, their nails grow very quickly and require frequent clipping.

# IRISH WOLFHOUND

## PHYSICAL CHARACTERISTICS

Like other sight hounds, the Irish wolfhound is strong and muscular. These dogs have well-arched necks, long heads, deep chests, and large, dark eyes. They are also the tallest of all dog breeds. They can reach 32 inches in height and weigh between 120 and 155 pounds.

The Irish wolfhound's coat is a rough, harsh steel gray. It is especially wiry and long over the eyes and under the jaw.

## PERSONALITY

Irish wolfhounds are classic gentle giants. Calm, sensitive, and sweet, they are loyal companions who love to snuggle. Although their large size can make them seem intimidating, they are often considered too serene and accepting of strangers to make good guard dogs.

## HISTORY

Irish wolfhounds were found in Ireland as early as 400 BCE. Irish chieftains and kings used these sight hounds to hunt wolves and wild boar (which gave them the name "wolfhound"). Later, this powerful breed became the mascot of the Irish Guards and the Celtic symbol for strength and courage.

Since the early 1900s, their peaceful nature has enabled them to make the transition from hunting dog to faithful family companion. Despite their size, they make excellent therapy dogs due to their gentle and sensitive temperament.

## DID YOU KNOW?

- Irish wolfhounds were used in Scotland for herding sheep. Many who use Irish wolfhounds for herding say that this breed is best at it—even better than the most famous herder, the border collie.

- Irish wolfhounds almost became extinct. Thankfully, they were brought back from extinction by crossbreeding wolfhounds with deerhounds, Great Danes, and mastiffs.

## Caretaking Tips

Despite the breed's double coat, grooming is low maintenance and there is very little shedding. A thorough weekly brushing is more than enough.

Irish wolfhounds are highly active and need daily exercise to keep them happy and healthy. Long walks, vigorous play sessions, and canine sports are all wonderful outlets. A secured area is necessary because, like all hounds, they may be prone to chase after a scent.

Irish wolfhounds are fast learners and crave the company of their people. This makes the breed highly trainable.

# RHODESIAN RIDGEBACK

### PHYSICAL CHARACTERISTICS

Ridgebacks have a muscular, athletic build. Males are about 26 inches tall and weigh 80 to 90 pounds. Females are around 25 inches tall and 65 to 75 pounds.

Their sleek, short coat is a beautiful red wheaten color, with white markings on their chest and toes. However, it is the eye-catching ridge of hair down their backs that distinguishes this breed and gives them their name. The distinctive ridge is formed by the hair growing in the opposite direction to the rest of the coat.

### PERSONALITY

Ridgebacks are a complex breed. They are strong-willed, loyal, brave, and protective. However, they also have a gentler side that is kind, affectionate, and completely devoted to their family. They are tolerant and do not bark unnecessarily. They tend to bark only as a warning, making them excellent watchdogs.

### HISTORY

The roots of the Rhodesian ridgeback can be traced back as early as the 1500s. Europeans brought several dog breeds to South Africa. They bred these dogs with the "ridged-back" dogs that native African people used for hunting.

In 1877, ridgebacks were brought to Rhodesia, the country now known as Zimbabwe, where they were raised and

**DID YOU KNOW?**
Ridgebacks are surprisingly good with cats if brought up with them.

further developed to hunt big game. The resulting breed was used in packs to hunt lions.

The breed arrived in the United States in the early to mid-1900s. Today it has become a faithful family companion.

## Caretaking Tips

The Rhodesian ridgeback is a highly intelligent and active breed who needs to be kept busy. Daily outings, long walks, play sessions, and canine sports are all wonderful ways to keep them engaged and satisfied.

The breed loves to run but is notorious for getting into mischief when off leash. Therefore, off-leash exercise and play should only take place in a secured area.

Grooming needs are simple. Their coat only needs basic care. Brush every other day and bathe monthly.

**CHAPTER 3**

# WORKING GROUP

**Working dogs are a** diverse group skilled in several different jobs. Their natural instincts have been carefully sharpened with breeding to perform practical tasks, such as protecting people or livestock, pulling carts or sleds, and performing search and rescue missions. Many also serve as police, military, and service dogs. Today, many have also become solid family companions and watchdogs.

Breeds in this group are primarily large, powerful dogs known for being robust, hardworking, highly intelligent, and loyal. They are also naturally protective of their families, so early and proper training and socialization is essential.

# BERNESE MOUNTAIN DOG

## PHYSICAL CHARACTERISTICS

Bernese mountain dogs, or Berners, are striking, with a powerful, sturdy build and a broad head and chest. The breed's long, silky tricolor coat is jet black, clear white, and rust. They also have distinctive markings, including a white blaze on the head, white markings on the chest, and reddish-brown markings extending down to their feet. Their gorgeous coat, along with the charming gleam in their eyes, makes this breed simply irresistible.

Males are 26 inches tall and 90 to 120 pounds. Females are slightly smaller, at 25 inches tall and 70 to 100 pounds.

## PERSONALITY

In addition to being notably beautiful, this breed has a lovely temperament. The dogs' kind, gentle, patient, and friendly manner make them an affectionate and loyal companion. They are also highly intelligent, alert, and deeply devoted to and protective of their families.

## HISTORY

The Bernese mountain dog originated in Switzerland, near the city of Bern (for which it is named), where the breed was an all-purpose farm dog. They guarded farmlands and livestock and served as gentle companions when the work of the day was done.

### DID YOU KNOW?

- These good-natured dogs have a sense of humor. If they find a particular antic or action makes their people laugh, they are bound to repeat it. This is known as the "Berner chuckle."

- The breed is known for its strength. Berners can haul up to 1,000 pounds—10 times their weight!

In the early 1900s, Professor Albert Heim saved the breed from extinction after many other working breeds were imported to Switzerland and breeding slowed down. They again became favored farm dogs and household companions.

Today, there are sponsored events that test the working ability of the breed, but this pales in comparison to their popular role as a faithful family companion.

## Caretaking Tips

Berners are active dogs and need at minimum 30 minutes of daily moderate exercise. They love outdoor activities, especially with their people, so they make excellent companions on long walks or hikes. They are naturals at canine sports like carting and drafting, in which dogs pull a cart or wagon, but also may enjoy herding, agility, and tracking. Their intelligent nature and eager-to-please attitude make them highly trainable.

Daily brushing and biweekly to monthly grooming will be necessary to keep their long double coat healthy and shiny.

# BOXER

### PHYSICAL CHARACTERISTICS

Boxers have compact, muscular bodies, forward thrusting jaws, a short and blunt muzzle, high-set ears (that are sometimes cropped), and an almost clownish, expressive face with dark brown eyes and a wrinkled forehead. Their tail is usually set high and docked.

These dogs are medium in build, with males reaching 23 to 25 inches tall and weighing 65 to 80 pounds. Females are 21 to 23 inches tall and weigh about 60 pounds. Their movements are much like the athletes they were supposedly named for: smooth, graceful, and powerful.

The boxer's short, smooth coat comes in fawn, brindle, and white. White is the only color not considered standard by the AKC.

## PERSONALITY

Boxers have big personalities. They are high-spirited, affectionate, deeply loyal, and very playful, making them endearing and entertaining family companions. Their comical nature is balanced by their courageous and protective side, which also makes them excellent guard dogs.

## HISTORY

 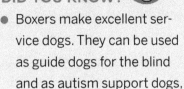
The boxer was developed in Germany in the 19th century. Their ancestry is believed to include other breeds, such as the bulldog and Great Dane.

This strong and powerful breed was originally used in bullbaiting, cart pulling, and hunting large game like wild boar. Today, boxers are used by police and the military for search and rescue missions and guard work. However, their most popular role is as a cherished family companion.

### Caretaking Tips

Plenty of daily exercise is a must for this high-energy breed. They are bouncy dogs that like to jump up on people, so early training is a must.

Grooming needs are minimal. Their short, shiny coat only requires a good once-over a couple of times a week. Boxers tend to be clean dogs, so only an occasional bath is needed.

# GREAT DANE

### PHYSICAL CHARACTERISTICS

A Great Dane is a giant, majestic breed. Its massive head, long-arched neck, and sleek, muscular body create an awe-inspiring appearance. Its ears can be left floppy or cropped. These dogs reach a whopping 30 to 32 inches tall and weigh 100 to 120 pounds. Their short, smooth coat comes in a variety of color patterns: brindle, fawn, blue, black, or harlequin (black patches over a white background).

### PERSONALITY

Great Danes are some of the best-natured dogs around. Aptly nicknamed the Gentle Giant, they are sweet, affectionate, patient, and deeply devoted family companions with a playful and peaceful disposition. However, do not let their soft side fool you. They can also be very protective of their family under the right circumstances.

### HISTORY

Funnily enough, the Great Dane is German in origin, not Danish. The breed has been around for about 400 years and was bred by German nobility to hunt wild boar and protect country estates.

Today, they still act as guard dogs. However, their primary role is as family companion. Since their exercise needs

**DID YOU KNOW?**

- Great Danes grow fast. They weigh about 1 or 2 pounds when born and can reach about 100 pounds by the time they are six months old.

- Great Danes were thought to ward off ghosts and evil spirits, which is why Scooby Doo (a Great Dane) was the perfect companion in the classic cartoon.

are surprisingly moderate given their size, they have even become popular with city dwellers who keep them as pets to deter robbers.

# MASTIFF

## PHYSICAL CHARACTERISTICS

The sheer size of the mastiff is a sight to behold. The breed has a large, broad head, drooping jowls, and a wrinkled forehead. A black mask around its wide-set eyes and muzzle is a beautiful accent to its coat of fawn, apricot, or brindle.

Mastiffs are one of the largest and heaviest dog breeds. They can grow to at least 31 inches tall and weigh as much as 175 to 220 pounds. Females reach at least 28 inches in height and weigh 150 to 190 pounds.

## PERSONALITY

Mastiffs are a noble and good-natured breed. They are surprisingly easygoing and patient for a guardian breed and make loyal family pets. However, this loyalty also makes them very protective of their family.

## HISTORY

The mastiff's ancestral roots can be traced back to ancient times. There are depictions of the breed on Egyptian monuments and mentions by Caesar when he invaded Britain around 55 BCE.

### DID YOU KNOW?

- The mastiff is known for producing large litters of 10 to 12 puppies. A mastiff set the record for the highest number of puppies in a single litter (24).

- A mastiff broke the record in the *Guinness Book of World Records* in 1987 for being the heaviest dog ever to live. Zorba weighed 314.5 pounds. He broke his own record two years later when he gained another 29 pounds!

The breed, as we know it, dates to medieval England, when they were used as big game hunters, estate guardians, and war dogs. A mastiff reportedly came to America on the *Mayflower*. Here the breed was developed to be more peaceful and friendlier than its ancestors.

### Caretaking Tips

Exercise requirements for this breed are moderate. Mastiffs tend to be more couch potatoes than athletes. However, regular exercise in the form of daily walks will keep them fit and healthy. Early training and socialization are advised to lessen the breed's guarding tendencies.

Grooming is simple. Their short coat looks fine with weekly brushings.

# ROTTWEILER

### PHYSICAL CHARACTERISTICS

The rottweiler is a large, muscular, rugged dog with a broad head, deep chest, docked tail, and overall imposing presence. Their short, shiny black coat is accented with striking tan markings on their legs, chest, and head.

They are slightly longer than they are tall, reaching about 26 inches tall and weighing about 85 to 135 pounds.

### PERSONALITY

Rottweilers are courageous and confident dogs who are highly active and intelligent. When well-bred and socialized early, they can make fun playmates and devoted family members. In fact, they crave attention and can be downright silly with their loved

ones. However, training is necessary to harness their easily aroused protective nature in a positive way.

## HISTORY

Believed to have descended from mastiff-like dogs of ancient Rome, rottweilers were named after the German cattle town of Rottweil, where they worked driving cattle, pulling carts, and guarding outposts.

When their time herding livestock ended, they found new work as police dogs, personal protectors, therapy dogs, and even search and rescue dogs. Their hardworking nature has made them increasingly popular as a family companion, reaching number eight on the AKC's most popular breeds list for 2020.

**DID YOU KNOW?**

- Rottweilers served as rescue dogs in New York after 9/11 alongside German shepherds and Labrador retrievers.

- Rottweilers were once herding dogs and still have a habit of bumping into people when they want them to fall in line. They also enjoy leaning their big bodies up against their people to show affection.

## Caretaking Tips

Rottweilers do best when given vigorous daily exercise. They love swimming, walking, and running, especially with their people. They also thrive when they have a job to do, such as herding, tracking, or retrieving. Early socialization and ongoing training are essential to focus their protective instincts in a positive way.

Grooming needs are relatively minimal. Regular bathing and weekly brushing are all this breed needs to stay happy and healthy.

# ST. BERNARD

## PHYSICAL CHARACTERISTICS

St. Bernards are massive, muscular dogs. They stand up to 30 inches tall and weigh up to 200 pounds.

Their huge head features a wrinkled brow, dark, droopy eyes, pronounced jowls, and an overall friendly expression.

St. Bernards have two types of coats: rough and smooth. Their coloring is white with markings in tan, red, mahogany, brindle, or black. Many have striking dark masks over their face.

## PERSONALITY

Saints, as they are affectionately called, are calm, patient, and instinctively friendly, making them wonderful family dogs. Despite their warm temperament, they are quick to protect family members if a situation arises.

## HISTORY

St. Bernards are an iconic breed whose lifesaving abilities are legendary. In 1050 CE, a monk named St. Bernard de Menthon, whom the breed is named after, established a hospice along the Alpine pass between Switzerland and Italy, where the breed proved to be the ideal rescue dog.

Their senses could predict incoming avalanches and

### DID YOU KNOW?

- The St. Bernard is often depicted wearing a barrel of brandy around its neck, supposedly to help cold travelers warm up. They never actually wore these miniature barrels on rescue missions, but they did carry packs filled with water and food.

- Due to their droopy jowls, St. Bernards tend to drool a lot, especially when they're hungry or hot.

detect a body buried under 20 feet of snow. They could dig the person out and then use their body to keep them warm until help arrived. From approximately 1697 to 1897, St. Bernards are credited with saving well over 2,000 human lives.

Today, they are mostly known as devoted family companions.

## Caretaking Tips

Despite their size and power, St. Bernards only require a moderate amount of exercise, like a long walk or play session. Early socialization and training are essential with a dog this size. Thankfully, their kindheartedness and eagerness to please make them highly trainable.

Grooming is the same for short- and longhaired varieties. An occasional bath and daily brushing during shedding season is needed. Be careful not to overbathe them, as it can strip their water-resistant coat of its necessary oils.

# SIBERIAN HUSKY

### PHYSICAL CHARACTERISTICS

The Siberian husky is an athletic, graceful dog developed for great endurance in cold temperatures. The breed's fox-like head, bushy tail, and thick coat give a striking, wolflike appearance. However, it is their remarkable eyes, in either brown, blue, or one of each, that have become the breed's trademark. The husky is a medium-size dog that ranges from 20 to 23.5 inches tall and weighs 35 to 60 pounds.

### PERSONALITY

Huskies are energetic, sociable, friendly dogs that enjoy the comfort and companionship of home and family. They are incredibly loyal and thrive on human company. Like many working breeds, they are independent thinkers and require firm but gentle training right from puppyhood.

### HISTORY

The breed's ancestors were developed 3,000 years ago by the Chukchi people of northeast Asia for use as sled pullers. However, in 1925, the fame of the Siberian husky as the ultimate sled dog was cemented when a team of huskies raced 340 miles through extreme weather to deliver lifesaving serum for a diphtheria outbreak in

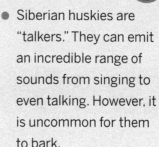

**DID YOU KNOW?**

- Siberian huskies are "talkers." They can emit an incredible range of sounds from singing to even talking. However, it is uncommon for them to bark.

- Siberian huskies are built for the cold. Their thick double coat serves as insulation and their almond-shaped eyes allow them to squint to keep out the snow.

Nome, Alaska. Huskies are still used as sled dogs for fun and sport. However, the breed's most popular role is as a beloved family companion.

### Caretaking Tips

Huskies are athletic, intelligent dogs with incredible endurance and a need to perform a task. Therefore, daily vigorous exercise is essential. They are also notorious escape artists, so a secured exercise area is necessary.

Grooming needs are minimal. Huskies are considered a natural breed (one developed without the intervention of people) and are remarkably self-cleaning. They only need occasional baths and brushing.

**CHAPTER 4**

## TERRIER GROUP

**This group was initially** bred to hunt small animals, like rats and foxes, as well as guard the family home and barn. They are smart, independent workers with keen eyesight and a relentless bark. Known to be fearless in spirit with a feisty persistence, they come in all shapes and sizes. The shorter-legged terriers, known as earth dogs, were bred to burrow underground in pursuit of rodents. The longer-legged varieties were also exterminators but bred to stay aboveground and dig out larger animals like badgers or foxes. Today, these spunky dogs make fun-loving companions, confident competitors, and courageous watchdogs.

# AIREDALE TERRIER

## PHYSICAL CHARACTERISTICS

The Airedale terrier is sturdy and strong, standing about 23 inches tall and weighing between 40 and 50 pounds. The breed has a classic long, flat head, a sporty beard and mustache, and dark, soulful eyes. Their dense, wiry coat is tan with black markings.

## PERSONALITY

Airedales form close bonds with their people. They are lively, confident, sociable, and full of character. They are gentle and patient with family, but equally fierce and protective of their home.

Intelligent and independent, the breed does not tolerate boredom and will get into mischief when left to their own devices. However, when mentally engaged, their spirit and sense of humor make them entertaining companions.

## HISTORY

The Airedale terrier can trace its lineage back to the now-extinct black and tan terrier. These terriers were bred to hunt vermin of all sizes. However, they lacked the scenting and swimming skills hunters desired, so in the 1800s, near the River Aire in Yorkshire, they were crossbred

### DID YOU KNOW?

- Airedales are famous for their bravery. In addition to their work in the British military during World War I, they were also among the very first breeds to be used for police work in England and Germany.

- Many Airedales have resided in the White House. Presidents Woodrow Wilson, Warren Harding, and Calvin Coolidge all had Airedale terriers.

with other breeds (like otterhounds and probably Irish and bull terriers) to create today's Airedale.

Airedales served in the British Armed Forces in World War I as messengers and guard dogs. In the United States, they became known as all-around great hunting dogs. The breed's versatility is legendary. Its many roles include rat hunter, duck dog, big-game hunter, herder, guardian, K-9 cop, and companion.

## Caretaking Tips

This boisterous breed needs to channel its energy into safe outlets. Several daily walks and active play sessions are usually enough to satisfy Airedales. The Airedales' intelligence and family devotion make them highly trainable. However, they bore easily, so varied training sessions will be more successful than repetitive ones.

Grooming needs are moderate. Weekly brushing and full grooming three or four times a year is sufficient to keep Airedales looking and feeling their best.

# AMERICAN STAFFORDSHIRE TERRIER

## PHYSICAL CHARACTERISTICS

American Staffordshire terriers are star athletes from head to tail. Their broad head and powerful jaws would seem intimidating if not for their famously goofy smiling expressions. AmStaffs, as they are affectionately called, stand about 19 inches tall and weigh anywhere from 45 to 70 pounds. The breed's short, glossy coat comes in many colors, including black, brown, and gray.

## PERSONALITY

When responsibly bred, well-socialized AmStaffs are affectionate, gentle, and playful. They simply love to love and are happiest when spending time cuddling with their people. Deeply loyal, they can be protective of their family, but otherwise they are friendly, docile, and good-natured.

The ancestors of the American Staffordshire terrier came from England and were a mix of bulldogs and terriers. They were used to manage bulls and hunt wild boars.

The breed was brought to America in the late 1800s for use on farms. Then known as the Staffordshire terrier, it was registered by the AKC in 1936. It changed names in 1972 to the American Staffordshire terrier to differentiate it from the Staffordshire bull terrier.

Today's AmStaff is mellower than their ancestors and continues to be an American favorite. Although some act as watchdogs or help with police work, their best role is as family companion.

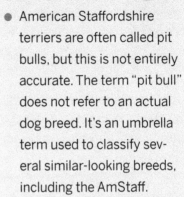

**DID YOU KNOW?**

- American Staffordshire terriers are often called pit bulls, but this is not entirely accurate. The term "pit bull" does not refer to an actual dog breed. It's an umbrella term used to classify several similar-looking breeds, including the AmStaff.

- Despite their tough appearance, AmStaffs aren't the best guard dogs. They are too friendly and usually greet strangers as they would friends.

## Caretaking Tips

The AmStaff is an energetic, sociable dog who thrives on long walks, runs, and vigorous play sessions with their family.

Early training and socialization are a must for this breed. Even well-socialized AmStaffs can still be reactive to other dogs, so supervision and caution must always be exercised.

Minimal grooming is needed. Only occasional brushing and bathing is needed to maintain the breed's wash-and-wear coat.

# BEDLINGTON TERRIER

## PHYSICAL CHARACTERISTICS

Bedlington terriers are one of the most recognizable breeds due to their striking resemblance to a lamb. Their fleecy, pear-shaped head, velvety, tasseled ears, and curvy contours make this breed unmistakable. Their body is both willowy and muscular, averaging between 17 and 23 pounds and 15 to 16 inches tall.

Their crisp, curly coat is a unique (and hypoallergenic) mixture of hard and soft hair and comes in several colors, including sandy, liver, and blue.

## PERSONALITY

Bedlington terriers can be gentle, affectionate, playful, and entertaining companions. However, they also have an alert and courageous side, making them fierce watchdogs who rarely back down from a challenge. The Bedlington terrier is truly a "graceful terrier in sheep's clothing."

### DID YOU KNOW?

The Bedlington terrier is virtually shed proof. At birth, their coat is very dark and becomes much lighter with maturity. If the dog sustains an injury that damages the coat, that spot grows back black.

## HISTORY

The breed first emerged in the early 19th century in the Bedlington parish of Northumberland, England.

Hunters used the breed to hunt and retrieve vermin. Over time, these terriers made their way into the homes of the elite, where they became first-class companions, a role they still enjoy today.

## Caretaking Tips

Bedlingtons are energetic and require daily exercise to stay healthy. They love long walks, runs, and playing fetch with their people. Due to their high prey drive, all exercise should be in a secure area.

Early training and socialization are important with this breed. Thankfully, they are highly trainable due to their intelligence and eagerness to please. Their strong hunting instincts call for special attention in teaching the dog to come consistently around intense distractions, as well as being comfortable around small animals.

Despite the lack of shedding, their coat requires bimonthly clippings and brushing at least twice a week.

# JACK RUSSELL TERRIER

## PHYSICAL CHARACTERISTICS

The Jack Russell is a small, courageous hunting terrier with a compact body, button ears that are folded forward, and dark almond-shaped eyes. The breed weighs between 13 and 17 pounds and stands between 13 and 14 inches tall. Their double, waterproof coat comes in white with black, tan, or black and tan markings. It is either smooth (short), rough (long/wiry), or broken (a mixture of both).

## PERSONALITY

Jack Russells are upbeat, curious, and clever dogs with a strong desire to work. Their high prey drive, low tolerance for boredom, and fondness for digging also make them a bit of a handful. However, with the right training, they can make loyal, entertaining companions.

## HISTORY

The Jack Russell terrier is a true working terrier dating back to 19th century England. The breed is named for avid hunter Reverend (Parson) John Russell, who developed it for hunting foxes.

In the 1930s, the breed gained popularity in the United States. Several breed clubs emerged, but they could not agree on what the breed should look like. Two clubs (one being the AKC) went in different directions. They knew having the same breed name would be confusing, so the Jack Russell Club went with the name Jack Russell terrier, and the AKC renamed their version of the breed the Parson Russell Terrier.

## Caretaking Tips

Jack Russells have limitless energy. Long walks, runs, or hikes are a necessity for keeping this breed satisfied and out of trouble. Creativity, patience, and a sense of humor will be needed in training your Jack Russell. Consider trick training, such as teaching your dog to "give paw" or "roll over," to keep training entertaining. Training will not eliminate this breed's prey drive, so keep them away from other family pets like cats and only exercise them in a secure area.

Grooming needs depend on a Jack Russell's coat type. The smooth coat does fine with weekly brushings. The broken or rough coat will require more grooming with a dog comb. Be aware that this breed's coat sheds a lot and is sun sensitive.

# MINIATURE SCHNAUZER

## PHYSICAL CHARACTERISTICS

The miniature schnauzer has a small but sturdy body and a rectangular head, with a signature walrus-like mustache and bushy eyebrows. These features make it one of the most recognizable breeds around. They stand between 13 and 14 inches tall and weigh between 10 and 18 pounds. Their hard, wiry coat comes most commonly in salt and pepper, but also in solid black or black and silver.

## PERSONALITY

Mini schnauzers are extroverts who love to be in the middle of the action. They are cheerful, curious, clever, and affectionate, with just the right amount of spunk to keep life interesting. Highly sociable, they love nothing more than being with their people and make fun family companions.

Miniature schnauzers were first bred in Germany in the late 19th century, where they became popular rat hunting dogs. They were also sometimes paired with German shepherds to keep livestock safe. The schnauzer's keen hearing and loud barking alerted the shepherd when there was trouble. They are descendants of affenpinschers and standard schnauzers and the only terrier breed without British ancestry.

In 1926, the AKC officially recognized the miniature schnauzer. The breed's ratting days are now over, and today these dogs are known as charming companions, frequent winners at dog shows, and one of the country's most popular breeds.

**DID YOU KNOW?**

The breed's distinct mustache isn't just for show. The thick facial hair was sometimes matted down into thick armor, which protected their face from retaliation from their prey.

## Caretaking Tips

This active breed benefits from regular daily exercise, preferably in a secured area where their prey drive can't lead them to run off. Miniature schnauzers are merry, bright dogs that are eager to please and highly trainable. However, they do not do well with repetition, so training needs to be fun and interesting.

The breed's double coat consists of a wiry topcoat and a soft undercoat. It rarely sheds but does require frequent brushing and professional trimming to look its best.

# SCOTTISH TERRIER

## PHYSICAL CHARACTERISTICS

This short-legged terrier is a solidly compact dog with a distinctive beard, bushy eyebrows, and a high-set tail. There is very little variation in size in the breed. All Scottish terriers are about 10 inches tall and weigh between 18 and 22 pounds.

Their wiry topcoat and soft, dense undercoat come primarily in black, although brindle and wheaten coats are sometimes seen. When untrimmed, the outer coat brushes the ground like a long skirt.

## PERSONALITY

Scottish terriers, or Scotties, are bold, independent, confident, and clever. They have a serious, independent nature and make good companions for those who can manage their feisty tendencies. Their wariness of strangers also makes them excellent watchdogs.

## HISTORY

The Scottish terrier dates to the 1700s, but the development of the breed as we know it today came about in the late 1800s. The Scottie originated in Aberdeen, Scotland, and was initially called the Aberdeen terrier. It was bred to hunt foxes, badgers, rabbits, and other small, den-dwelling animals.

The breed was first introduced in the United States

### DID YOU KNOW?

- The Scottish terrier comes in second for total number of Westminster Dog Show wins, with a total of 8 wins. The wire fox terrier has 15 wins.

- Three American presidents had Scotties: Presidents Dwight D. Eisenhower, Franklin D. Roosevelt, and George W. Bush.

in 1883. During the 1930s and 1940s, the Scottie soared in popularity among movie stars, who fell in love with their spicy charm. The breed gained even more fame when the nation was introduced to President Franklin Delano Roosevelt's beloved Scottie, Fala.

## Caretaking Tips

Scotties are active and need plenty of exercise. A good walk or a vigorous game of fetch or tug of war will keep them happy and in shape. They are highly intelligent and were bred to figure things out independently. As a result, training sessions work best when they are short, creative, and varied.

Regular grooming is required for this breed. If the coat is kept long, it will need brushing two or three times a week. If clipped it requires professional trimming every couple of months.

# WEST HIGHLAND WHITE TERRIER

## PHYSICAL CHARACTERISTICS

This short-legged terrier is a hardy, agile little dog with a sturdy, compact body, sharply pointed ears, dark, piercing eyes, and the overall appearance of a cute stuffed animal. Though small in stature, at 10 or 11 inches tall and 14 to 20 pounds, Westies, as they are affectionately called, are definitely not short on confidence or looks. Their rough snow-white coats are perhaps their most distinctive feature.

## PERSONALITY

Westies are lively, intelligent, spunky dogs with a genuine zest for life. Their happy, friendly, bold, and amusing nature makes them a family favorite, but it can also lead them into mischief. Ultimately, life with a Westie is never boring.

West Highland white terriers originated in northwestern Scotland in the 1700s. They were used to hunt rats and other vermin. They would also go with hunters on fox and rabbit hunts, flushing the game from their burrows.

It is believed that the Westie came from the same family tree as the Skye, Scottish, and cairn terriers, with different people selectively breeding them for different colors. White dogs were favored because they were easy to spot and distinguish from the prey they were hunting.

Today, they are primarily favored as family companions.

**DID YOU KNOW?**

Westies are built for tight spaces, but even they occasionally get stuck. Fortunately, they were bred to have an extra sturdy tail, allowing hunters to pull them out of holes. They were also bred to have a big bark so hunters could hear them barking underground. This is also helpful if they get stuck.

## Caretaking Tips

Westies' high energy and up-for-anything attitude make canine sports and adventure walks perfect outlets for them. These terriers will chase anything, so be sure to have them on leash or in a secure area. True of any terrier breed, they are intelligent but have an independent streak. Therefore, socialization and training should be done early and kept interesting. Special attention should be given to address digging and barking.

Regular grooming is necessary to keep Westies looking their best. Daily brushing and combing along with a trip to the groomer every four to six weeks is ideal.

# CHAPTER 5

# TOY GROUP

**Dogs in this group** may be short in stature, but they are big in personality. Unlike other groups, they were not bred to work. Instead, they were bred to be affectionate and devoted companions. They enjoy nothing more than being in constant close contact with their people, earning them the label of lapdogs. They are highly sociable, and their small size and portability make them adaptable to a variety of living situations and lifestyles. However, don't let their size, cuteness, and charming expressions fool you. They are also highly intelligent, feisty, and can have strong protective instincts.

# CAVALIER KING CHARLES SPANIEL

### PHYSICAL CHARACTERISTICS

These all-around beauties will draw you in with their large dark eyes, gentle expressions, and feathered tails that never stop wagging. One of the largest toy breeds, they stand between 12 or 13 inches tall and range between 10 and 18 pounds. Their silky coat comes in four color combinations: red and white (called Blenheim), black and tan, ruby (red), and tricolor (black and white with tan points).

### PERSONALITY

Cavalier King Charles spaniels are some of the sweetest dogs you will ever meet. Delightfully playful, outgoing, and affection-ate, they are deeply devoted to their people and love to cuddle, as well as go on long walks and hikes. They are highly adaptable to any lifestyle and are very popular family dogs. Their loving personality also makes them wonderful therapy dogs.

### HISTORY

Cavalier King Charles spaniels were originally bred to warm royal laps in drafty castles and on chilly carriage rides. King Charles I and his son King Charles II of England took such a fancy to them that the breed was named after them.

**DID YOU KNOW?**

Although its history goes back centuries, today's Cavalier is considered relatively new. The AKC did not recognize the breed until 1995.

Cavaliers came to the United States from England in the 1940s. Their popularity has risen since 2000, and today they rank 17th on the AKC's most popular breed list.

## Caretaking Tips

Although this breed is quite content in their role as beloved lapdog, they also enjoy walks and other outdoor activities. Moderate exercise is helpful in keeping them at a healthy weight. However, they are not "street savvy" and tend to be unaware of their surroundings, especially when following a scent, so always keep them on a leash or in a secure area. Cavaliers are highly intelligent and eager to please, making them highly trainable. Because they always want to be with their people, it is important to focus on training that builds their comfort level with being alone.

   Their silky coat requires regular brushing and an occasional bath to keep it in healthy condition.

# CHIHUAHUA

### PHYSICAL CHARACTERISTICS

Chihuahuas are the smallest dogs in the world, standing only between 7 and 9 inches tall and weighing as little as 2 pounds and rarely more than 6 pounds. Their rounded "apple" head is a breed hallmark. They have large, erect ears and expressive, luminous eyes. Their coats can be long or short and come in almost any color or pattern.

### PERSONALITY

Chihuahuas are tiny dogs with a huge personality and big-dog attitude. They are bold, confident, and clever with an almost terrier-like demeanor. Their alert nature and wariness of

strangers make them excellent watchdogs. They often bond strongly to one person, but they can make new friends if properly introduced. Chihuahuas have a sensitive side and thrive on affection and companionship.

## HISTORY

There are several theories regarding the Chihuahua's lineage, but regardless of its ancient history, the shorthaired Chihuahua we know today was first noticed by Americans in the 1850s in the Mexican state of Chihuahua, for which the breed was named.

American visitors to Mexico brought the breed back to the United States, and in 1908 the AKC registered the breed. The longhaired variety was probably created from crosses with papillons and Pomeranians. Since the 1960s, the Chihuahua has been one of the most popular breeds registered by the AKC, a standing it still holds today.

### Caretaking Tips

Chihuahuas love to run and play, but overall, their exercise needs are minimal. Short, slow walks or a light game of fetch is usually enough to keep them happy and healthy.

This toy breed is highly intelligent and quite sassy. Therefore, early training and socialization are essential to creating a good-natured and well-mannered dog.

Grooming needs depend on coat type. The smooth, short coat needs only occasional brushing. The longer coat variety needs more attention with weekly brushing a priority to keep the coat tangle free.

# HAVANESE

## PHYSICAL CHARACTERISTICS

Havanese are small, sturdy, active dogs with drop ears and a high-set tail that curls over their backs. They stand between 10 and 11 inches tall and weigh 7 to 13 pounds.

Once called the *Blanquito de la Habana,* or "Havana Silk Dog," their gorgeous double coat feels like fine silk. It can be straight or wavy and comes in many colors.

## PERSONALITY

Havanese are cuddly, gentle, and affectionate dogs that thrive on being at the center of attention. They are also curious in nature, highly intelligent, and playful. Their easygoing temperament and love of human companionship make them ideal family dogs as well as wonderful therapy dogs.

**DID YOU KNOW?**

Havanese are easily recognized by their "springy" gait, a result of having strong back legs and relatively short front legs.

## HISTORY

This native lapdog of Cuban aristocrats dates back to the early 1500s, when Spanish settlers began to establish colonies in the New World. They brought with them their companion dogs, which were the ancestors of the Havanese we know today.

The breed was refined over the next 300 years. During that time, European travelers fell in love with the breed and brought the dogs back to England, Spain, and France. In 1959, Cubans fleeing Castro's revolution brought their dogs with them to the United States.

Today the breed is a popular choice for a family companion.

## Caretaking Tips

Havanese are energetic little dogs, but a long daily walk or an active game of fetch is enough to keep them happy. This breed is smart and eager to please, making them highly trainable. Special focus should be given to building their comfort level for being left alone. Early socialization is also essential. Calmly expose them to new places and people at an early age.

Routine grooming is required to keep their silky coat healthy and tangle free. They should be brushed daily. Some owners choose to keep a shorter coat, which then requires monthly haircuts.

# POMERANIAN

### PHYSICAL CHARACTERISTICS

The tiny, adorable, fox-faced Pomeranian is striking with its glorious fluffy coat and heavily plumed tail. Pomeranians come in a variety of colors, although a rich red is most common. The Pomeranian is a true "toy" breed, standing 10 or 11 inches tall and weighing only between 3 and 7 pounds.

### PERSONALITY

Although tiny in size, Poms, as they're affectionately nicknamed, have a commanding big-dog attitude. Their vivacious, perky personality makes these dogs entertaining and loving companions.

They are also highly intelligent, alert, and inquisitive.
Poms will bark at anything out
of the ordinary, which makes
them excellent watchdogs
as well.

## HISTORY

The Pomeranian is a miniaturized relation of the sled dogs of the
Arctic. The breed was named for the region Pomerania, now part
of Poland and western Germany. It was there, in the 1800s, that
the breed was bred to be smaller than their larger ancestors.

The Pom's popularity soared after Queen Victoria became
smitten with the breed. She is also credited for breeding the
size of the Pom down even further to the toy breed we know
today. The breed continues to be a favored companion, with
just the right amount of watchdog worked in.

### Caretaking Tips

Although Poms are happy to be lapdogs, they also benefit from
moderate exercise. They enjoy the chance to go on walks and to
run and play. They are known to be escape artists, so always keep
an eye on them when outside. Small in stature, Poms think they
are bigger than they are and do not hesitate to challenge bigger
dogs. Therefore, early socialization and training is essential. Thankfully, their keen intelligence and connection to their people make
them highly trainable. In fact, they thrive on learning tricks and
performing.

Pomeranians' most distinguishing feature is their luxurious double coat, which needs to be brushed one or two times
a week. Professional grooming every four to six weeks is also
recommended.

# PUG

### PHYSICAL CHARACTERISTICS

Pugs may be small, but they pack a lot of muscle onto their square frame. Their squishy face with prominent sparkling eyes and wrinkled brow exudes a variety of emotions, from surprise to curiosity. Two of their most distinguishable features are their short, blunt muzzle and their high-set curled tail. They stand between 10 and 14 inches tall and weigh in the range of 13 to 20 pounds. Their short, dense coat comes in two standard colors: fawn with a black mask or solid black.

### PERSONALITY

Playful, spirited, and rambunctious, pugs are the class clowns of the dog world. They are highly intelligent, often mischievous, and always charming. Pugs' affectionate, sociable, and attentive nature makes them loving and loyal family companions.

### HISTORY

An ancient breed dating back 2,000 years, pugs were once the treasured companions of Chinese emperors. They were considered good luck because their forehead wrinkles resembled the Chinese character for "prince." Then, in the 1500s and 1600s, Dutch traders brought the breed to Europe, where they gained popularity in royal households. They were especially popular during the Victorian era.

**DID YOU KNOW?**

Emperors of China treated their pugs to the luxuries of royal life. Sometimes the pampered pups were given their own mini palaces and guards.

The breed came to the United States after the Civil War and was recognized by the AKC in 1885. Today, this breed has a huge fan base and is a highly sought-after family companion.

## Caretaking Tips

Exercise needs are low, but it is wise to give pugs daily moderate exercise with walks and play sessions to keep them fit and healthy. Always remember that this short-faced breed does not tolerate hot weather. If temperatures rise, exercise inside.

Pugs are eager to please and generally easy to train. Like other companion breeds, they need early training that focuses on building their comfort level with being alone.

Grooming needs are minimal. Frequent bathing is not needed, but their facial creases must be cleaned regularly.

# SHIH TZU

### PHYSICAL CHARACTERISTICS

The beloved shih tzu is a hardy breed with a small, sturdy body, short snout, and prominent eyes. They stand 8 to 11 inches tall and weigh between 9 and 16 pounds. Their long, luxurious coat comes in 14 different colors. It is accented with a white tip on their plumed tail and a white blaze on their forehead.

### PERSONALITY

While shih tzu is the Mandarin phrase for "little lion," this breed is the quintessential companion dog thriving on human company. Shih tzus are renowned for their affectionate, happy, and perky personality and are quite content just sitting on laps and acting adorable.

### HISTORY

The shih tzu is one of the few breeds whose primary role has always been that of companion. The breed originated in Tibet around the 7th century. One theory is that the breed developed from a cross between the Pekingese (creating the breeds' shorter snout) and the smaller Lhasa apso-type dogs.

Shih tzus were given as gifts to Chinese royalty. When the British arrived in China, they brought the breed back to England. In the late 1940s and 1950s, US soldiers stationed in European countries brought the shih tzu home with them. Today, they continue to be one of the most beloved companion breeds.

**DID YOU KNOW?**
Tibetan monks considered shih tzus sacred. The breed acted as companions and alarm dogs. They were even trained to turn the prayer wheels during the Buddhist prayer rituals.

## Caretaking Tips

The shih tzu was primarily bred to be a house companion, so exercise needs are quite minimal. Playtime indoors and short walks seem to be enough to satisfy this breed. Shih tzus have a short snout, which makes them heat intolerant. They have a reduced ability to breathe in air, so they are more prone to their bodies overheating.

Their coats shed very little but do require extensive grooming. When kept long, daily brushing is required. To protect their sensitive eyes, the hair on their head needs to be trimmed or tied up. Shih tzus also look cute in a "puppy trim," or a coat that is cut short, which is easier to maintain.

# YORKSHIRE TERRIER

## PHYSICAL CHARACTERISTICS

Yorkshire terriers, or Yorkies, are among the smallest of all breeds. They are usually no more than 7 pounds and 8 inches tall. They have tiny heads, small, V-shaped ears, and dark, expressive eyes.

Yorkies' most striking feature is their long, fine, silky coat in steel blue or golden tan. It has a similar texture to human hair. This makes grooming time-consuming but cuts down on shedding. The long hair on the top of their head is sometimes tied up with a ribbon.

## PERSONALITY

Even with their "toy" stature, they have the energy, confidence, and feistiness of other terriers. They are spunky, smart, insatiably curious, and often mischievous, making them the classic "big dog in a small body." With proper handling, they also make for loving, loyal, and entertaining companions.

**DID YOU KNOW?**

A Yorkie named Smoky became famous for her heroic actions during World War II. In addition to entertaining soldiers and becoming known as "the first therapy dog," she is credited with dragging an important telegraph wire through a 70-foot-long, 8-inch-wide pipe!

## HISTORY

The Yorkshire terrier was first developed in Yorkshire, England, during the Victorian era. Originally, they were excellent ratters (dogs bred to chase rats) in English wool mills. In time, these ratters transformed into companions for aristocratic ladies and began appearing in dog shows as "fancy terriers."

Yorkies made their way to the United States in 1872 and quickly became a favorite. The breed continues to be one of the AKC's top 20 breeds year after year.

## Caretaking Tips

This spirited breed benefits from both physical and mental activities. Starting from an early age, they should be introduced to new people and other dogs in a slow and calm manner. Despite their small size, they have big "terrier" attitudes and can become overly cautious or on guard with new people or dogs if not properly socialized.

Grooming their gorgeous glossy coat is not for the faint of heart. If the coat is kept long, it needs to be brushed daily and their long top knot needs to be tied up and kept out of their eyes. Professional grooming will be a necessity, along with weekly bathing. Some owners opt for a puppy trim (as in the photo above), but this will still require daily brushing and regular trips to the groomer.

# CHAPTER 6

# NONSPORTING GROUP

**Nonsporting dogs are an** assorted group of breeds with a variety of shapes, sizes, coats, and temperaments. The only thing they seem to have in common is that they do not fit into any of the other AKC groups. They come from diverse backgrounds and places of origin. Some had a specific job at some point in history, like hunting, herding, or guarding. Now, however, they are primarily companion dogs. Others were specifically bred as companion dogs and served as specialty pets for nobility and royalty. Today, they continue to be affectionate lapdogs for a wider sector of the population.

# BOSTON TERRIER

## PHYSICAL CHARACTERISTICS

The Boston terrier is a compact, handsome little dog with a broad chest, pointed, bat-like ears, a short muzzle, and wide, round eyes. These dogs stand between 16 and 17 inches tall and are grouped into three weight categories: under 15 pounds, 15 to 20 pounds, and 20 to 25 pounds. Their most distinguishing feature is their short, smooth tuxedo-like coat in either black and white, white with brindle (light brown), or white with seal (dark brown).

## PERSONALITY

Boston terriers are lively, playful, and comical dogs and are one of the most popular family dogs around. They are a bright, people-oriented, and good-natured breed and make cheerful and affectionate companions. They are nicknamed the American Gentleman, due to their tuxedo-like markings and gentle nature.

## HISTORY

This breed was developed in Boston in the late 1800s by crossing bulldogs and white English terriers. Boston terriers are considered one of the few truly all-American breeds. They have been called several names over the decades, but in 1891, they officially became known as the Boston terrier, after

### DID YOU KNOW?

- Despite their name, these dogs are not technically terriers. The AKC excludes them from the terrier group and classifies them under the nonsporting group.

- The state of Massachusetts loves this breed so much that they officially made it the state dog on May 14, 1979.

the city where they were developed. The AKC registered the breed in 1893. To this day, the breed is a symbol of hometown pride and the official mascot of Boston University.

## Caretaking Tips

Boston terriers need daily exercise, but a few short walks or sessions of engaging play seem to be enough to satisfy the breed. They love nothing more than activities shared with family. Just remember, the breed's short snout makes them heat intolerant.

Grooming needs are minimal. Weekly brushing and an occasional bath are enough to keep them happy and healthy.

# DALMATIAN

### PHYSICAL CHARACTERISTICS

The dalmatian is a graceful, elegantly proportioned, dog with a sleek, muscular body. They are athletes of incredible stamina, bred to go the distance. They stand 19 to 23 inches tall and weigh between 45 and 60 pounds.

Dalmatians' short, dense white coat adorned with black or liver spots is one of the most distinctive and eye-catching coats of all dog breeds.

### PERSONALITY

Dalmatians are high-energy, alert, sensitive dogs who can be dignified one minute and goofy the next. They are smart with a

clever sense of humor and love to make their family laugh. Dalmatians are deeply devoted to their people and equally wary of strangers, making them excellent watchdogs as well as loyal family companions.

## HISTORY

The dalmatian's origin is relatively unknown but the breed takes its name from Dalmatia, a coastal area now known as Croatia.

The breed is most famously a "coach dog." In the 1800s, they would trot alongside carriages and coaches to protect them and the horses from other dogs and threats. Eventually, horses were used to pull fire engines, and this is where dalmatians began their long association with firefighters. Today, they are primarily family companions, although some firehouses across the country still have them as mascots.

### Caretaking Tips

These athletic dogs do best with regular exercise, such as vigorous games of fetch, jogging, and long hikes. They are sensitive and tend to be wary of the unfamiliar. Early training and socialization to create positive associations with new people and places is essential.

Dalmatians shed a great deal, but overall, their grooming needs are minimal to keep their unique coat in tip-top shape.

# ENGLISH BULLDOG

## PHYSICAL CHARACTERISTICS

This brawny powerhouse is an unmistakable breed with its muscular, low-slung body, short, stocky legs, thick neck, heavily wrinkled face, pushed-in snout, and undershot jaw. Their lower teeth slightly protrude, creating an almost comical grin. They stand between 16 and 17 inches tall and weigh between 50 and 54 pounds. Their short, smooth coat comes in a variety of colors and patterns, including brindle, red, and solid white.

## PERSONALITY

English bulldogs, known simply as bulldogs, are sweet, gentle, people-oriented dogs that actively seek out human attention. Their amusing antics and distinctive rolling gait cannot help but make one smile. Easygoing with just the right amount of dignified courage, they make loyal family companions as well as excellent watchdogs.

## HISTORY

The English bulldog seems to have originated in the British Isles sometime before the 13th century. They were used in the sport of bull baiting. After the sport was banned, the breed almost became extinct.

In the early 19th century, bulldog enthusiasts began breeding them to have kinder, gentler temperaments. Their transition from brawler to companion was a huge success, and today they are a highly popular companion breed.

### DID YOU KNOW?

- The bulldog has long been the national symbol of England. In America, the breed is also the mascot for Yale University, the University of Georgia's football team, and the US Marine Corps.

- Otto the Skateboarding Bulldog recently broke the Guinness World Record for "longest human tunnel traveled through by a skateboarding dog." Otto sailed under the legs of 30 people in Lima, Peru.

## Caretaking Tips

Bulldogs are happy to chill out and relax most of the time. However, moderate exercise, like walks, is best for keeping them healthy and trim. Like other short-muzzled breeds, they are heat intolerant and should never be left unsupervised around water because they cannot swim.

Despite being heavy shedders, their grooming needs are minimal. Brushing two or three times weekly is usually enough to keep their coat shiny and healthy. But, their pronounced facial wrinkles need to be cleaned regularly.

# FRENCH BULLDOG

## PHYSICAL CHARACTERISTICS

This compact, adorable breed packs a lot of power in a small body. Standing between 11 and 12 inches tall, French bulldogs are 25 to 27 pounds of pure muscle. Their most notable feature is their large "bat" ears that are wide at the base and rounded on top. Their unique anatomy makes it almost impossible for them to swim.

## PERSONALITY

Adorable looks are just part of the story. Frenchies, as they are affectionately called, are playful, charming, smart, and entertaining. Their fun-loving nature and their deep desire for human connection make them attentive and desirable family companions—it's no wonder they consistently rank in the top 10 of the most popular breeds.

### DID YOU KNOW?

Frenchies tend to not be active barkers. However, they do produce sounds like yawning, yipping, and even gargling. Many Frenchie families swear they have their own language.

## HISTORY

The French bulldog is a descendant of the English toy bulldog. They gained popularity with England's lacemakers of the mid-19th century, who kept the dogs to chase rats in the factories. These lacemakers later relocated to northern France and brought their dogs with them.

Over several decades, these dogs were crossed with other breeds (possibly terriers and pugs) and developed their infamous "bat" ears. In the late 1800s and early 1900s, the breed became known as a companion dog of high society. Today, the breed is popular as a companion dog all over the world.

## Caretaking Tips

French bulldogs need only moderate exercise to keep them fit and healthy. A short walk or outdoor play session easily satisfies their needs. Like other flat-faced breeds, they should not exercise in extreme heat and humidity.

The breed's freethinking nature may appear to be an obstacle in their training. However, they are very bright, people-pleasing dogs that respond well to training when it is done in a positive, fun manner.

The Frenchie's short coat sheds minimally and needs very little grooming. However, it is important that its facial folds be kept clean and dry.

# POODLE

## PHYSICAL CHARACTERISTICS

Poodles come in three varieties: standard (over 15 inches tall and 45 to 70 pounds), miniature (10 to 15 inches and 12 to 20 pounds), and toy (less than 10 inches and about 5 to 7 pounds). They all have the same build and proportions, with a smooth, muscled body, tapered muzzle, and dropped ears. The hallmark of the breed is their glorious coat, which is tight and curly and comes in a variety of colors.

## PERSONALITY

Poodles are a lively, playful, versatile breed. They are notorious for their intelligence and dignified personality, though they also have a goofy side. They are extremely loyal and make engaging family companions.

## HISTORY

The poodle is the national dog of France. Yet, it is Germany where the breed originated. The German word *pudelin,* from which the poodle takes its name, means "splashing in water." This is a fitting name for the talented retrieving water dog.

Poodles started out as hunting dogs, but soon their intelligent nature had them branching out into more performance roles. The aristocracy, specifically in France, discovered the breed and fell madly in love with their personality and gorgeous coat.

Today, they continue to be one of the most popular

**DID YOU KNOW?**

Poodles' flamboyant 'do is meant for function, not fashion. Less hair made them more efficient swimmers, while puffs of hair around their legs and upper body protected their joints and vital organs from the cold-water temperatures.

breeds in the world and are often bred with other popular breeds, like golden retrievers, Labradors, and Bernese mountain dogs, to create hypoallergenic "doodle" mixes.

### Caretaking Tips

Poodles of any size require an active lifestyle, with daily physical and mental exercise. They enjoy all kinds of activities, including long walks, swimming, jogging, and retrieving games. This is an extremely smart breed that is quick to please their people but will be just as quick to try and outsmart them if the opportunity arises.

Grooming is a fact of life for this breed. Poodles' coats tend to mat, so they need to be kept in a close clip or groomed daily. Either way, professional grooming is often necessary.

# SHIBA INU

### PHYSICAL CHARACTERISTICS

Shiba Inus have an almost fox-like appearance. Their upright ears, squinty eyes, curly tail, and alert expression make them easily distinguishable. They stand between 13 and 17 inches tall and weigh anywhere from 17 to 23 pounds. The breed's thick double coat is rich in texture and most commonly comes in orange-red, with white markings.

### PERSONALITY

Shiba Inus are bold, energetic, confident dogs with a mind of their own. Their strong-willed nature is tempered by their loyalty and affection for family and their ability to adapt to a variety of lifestyles. They are devoted companions, but they also make excellent watchdogs due to their wariness of strangers.

## HISTORY

The Shiba Inu is the oldest of Japan's breeds. The breed goes back to ancient times (300 BCE) when they were bred to hunt in the rugged mountains of Japan. *Shiba* means "brushwood" (referring to the brush in the mountains) and *Inu* means "dog" in Japanese.

The Shiba Inu is a relatively new breed in the United States. It was imported by an American military family in 1954. Today, they are the number-one companion breed in Japan. Over the last 50 years, they have also continued to gain popularity in this role in the United States.

### DID YOU KNOW?

- The Japanese have three words to describe this breed: *kan-I* (alert and brave), *ryosei* (good-natured and loyal), and *soboku* (natural good looks).

- The breed is notorious for the "Shiba Scream." They are known to let out a high-pitched wail to express their emotions.

### Caretaking Tips

Shiba Inus are an active breed that requires regular exercise. They are independent thinkers with a wariness toward strangers, so early training and socialization are necessary. Also, this breed should be kept on leash because their prey drive makes them unreliable in open areas.

The breed's thick, double coat does not tend to mat. However, it does shed profusely, so daily brushing or combing can be helpful in reducing the amount of hair around the house.

# XOLOITZCUINTLI
## (SHOW-LO-EATS-QUEENT-LY)

**PHYSICAL CHARACTERISTICS**

This graceful yet rugged breed comes in three sizes: toy (10 to 14 inches tall, 10 to 15 pounds), miniature (14 to 18 inches tall, 15 to 30 pounds), and standard (18 to 23 inches tall, 30 to 55 pounds).

All have a lean, muscular body, bat-like ears, a long, thin tail, and a wrinkled brow that gives them the appearance of being deep in thought. However, perhaps their most distinct characteristic is being hairless! They also come in a coated variety, though it's less popular.

## PERSONALITY

Xolos, as they are commonly called, are a smart and sensitive breed. They are aloof with strangers but extremely even-tempered, playful, and loyal to family members. Their alert, charming, and somewhat protective nature makes them equally loving companions and attentive watchdogs.

## HISTORY

The Xoloitzcuintli is a rare and very ancient breed, dating back at least 3,000 years. They are national treasures in Mexico and were considered sacred by the Aztecs, who named the breed after their dog-headed god, Xolotl.

Ancient people used these dogs for companionship, hunting, and protection. Today, the breed is both a watchdog and family companion.

### Caretaking Tips

Xolos are famously calm and laid-back at home and only need moderate exercise. Walks and upbeat play sessions are enough to satisfy their needs.

This breed takes their watchdog duties seriously, so early socialization to new people and places along with consistent training is recommended.

Both coated and hairless varieties have minimal grooming needs. The more common hairless variety only requires an occasional bath. However, they need sunscreen to protect their delicate skin from prolonged sun exposure.

**CHAPTER 7**

# HERDING GROUP

**Herding breeds were part** of the working group until 1983 and were specifically developed to gather, herd, and protect livestock. Consequently, these dogs have an instinctual ability to control the movement of animals. The herding instinct is so strong in these dogs that they have also been known to gently herd their families! They are exceptionally intelligent, have boundless energy, and are keenly responsive to training. Some, like the German shepherd and Belgian Malinois, are commonly used for police and protection work. Herding breeds also excel at canine sports, like agility, and make loyal and loving family companions.

# AUSTRALIAN SHEPHERD

## PHYSICAL CHARACTERISTICS

Australian shepherds, or Aussies, are an agile, medium-size breed with a solid build, penetrating gaze, and tireless work ethic. They stand 18 to 23 inches tall and weigh between 40 and 60 pounds.

Aussies are one of the most eye-catching breeds with their lush, medium-length coat and gorgeous blue or light-colored eyes. Coat colors can vary from blue or red merle (a coat with irregular color patches) to red or black tricolor. Their coats can have white, tan, or white-and-tan markings.

## PERSONALITY

Australian shepherds are highly intelligent, even-tempered, and exuberant dogs that are deeply loyal and protective of their families. They have an irresistible impulse to herd anything—from birds to dogs to kids—and thrive on having a job to do. They excel at canine sports and make loving and devoted family companions—assuming the family is an active one!

## HISTORY

The origins of the Australian shepherd date back to the Basque shepherds of Spain, who later immigrated to Australia and took their dogs with them. When the Basque shepherds came to the United States in the 1800s, Americans thought these dogs were of Australian origin and named the breed the Australian shepherd.

The breed as we know it today was bred solely in the United States and became an iconic part of cowboy culture herding livestock. Many still work as herding dogs or barn dogs in the American West, while others have found work as therapy or police dogs. They have also become a highly popular companion breed.

### Caretaking Tips

Australian shepherds do best with plenty of daily exercise and a job to perform, preferably in close partnership with their humans. Long walks, hikes, and canine sports are wonderful outlets for fulfilling their activity needs. The breed is easily trainable due to their high intelligence, loyalty to their family, and eagerness to work.

Aussies' thick, waterproof coat sheds year-round, but more so in the spring when they shed their winter coat. Weekly brushing, with added time in shedding season, should be enough to keep them healthy and mat free.

# BELGIAN MALINOIS

## PHYSICAL CHARACTERISTICS

The Belgian Malinois is a strong, well-proportioned breed that, at first glance, resembles a German shepherd. These dogs have a muscular build and look more elegant than bulky. They stand 22 to 24 inches tall and weigh between 40 and 75 pounds. Their short double coat comes in colors ranging from rich fawn to mahogany. Their distinctive black ears and mask accentuate their dark chocolate-colored eyes.

**DID YOU KNOW?**

Belgian Malinois are often used for skydiving military operations. They are just as smart as but lighter than German shepherds, so it is easier to use them for tandem jumps with their handlers. They can even be trained to jump on their own!

## PERSONALITY

Belgian Malinois are bold, confident working dogs known for their intelligence, energy, and the strong bond they form with their human partners. They are affectionate and protective of their family, making them loving companions and passionate but controlled watchdogs.

## HISTORY

Malinois were bred near the Belgian city of Malines. They are one of four closely related breeds of Belgian herding dogs. In some countries, these breeds are classified together. However, in the United States, they have been recognized as a separate breed since 1959.

Malinois were first bred as high-performance livestock herders, a role they continued when they came to the United States in 1911. However, their high work drive and versatility soon expanded their jobs to include police and military work. Today, they are also considered excellent guard dogs as well as beloved family companions.

### Caretaking Tips

Belgian Malinois are exceptionally athletic, intelligent, and devoted companions. Therefore, plenty of both physical and mental engagement is essential to their overall health and happiness.

Thankfully, they also are one of the most trainable breeds. Early training and socialization will be needed to temper their protective instincts and channel their herding and prey drives into more acceptable activities.

Grooming needs are minimal. Occasional brushing during most of the year with a daily once-over in shedding season is enough to keep their coat in good condition.

# BORDER COLLIE

## PHYSICAL CHARACTERISTICS

Border collies are muscular yet agile dogs with almost super-natural amounts of energy and stamina. The breed trademark is their intense stare (when approaching sheep), famously known as the border's "herding eye."

Looking like a lighter-weight Australian shepherd with a feathered tail, borders stand 21 or 22 inches tall and weigh 42 to 45 pounds. They have two coat varieties: smooth and rough.

## PERSONALITY

Borders are extremely bright workaholics with tireless energy, a low tolerance for boredom, and a high level of sensitivity to their handler's every cue. They need to be busy and thrive when they have a job to perform. They are often considered to be one of the most intelligent of dog breeds, due to their ability to learn an extensive number of words and commands.

### DID YOU KNOW?

This breed has broken all kinds of records. One border collie named Chaser is widely recognized as the world's smartest dog since she knows the names of more than 1,000 objects.

## HISTORY

Border collies date back to the 18th century in the rocky highlands of Scotland and England, where they were bred to herd sheep. Called the world's greatest herders for their speed, agility, and focus, borders have dominated competitive sheep-dog trials in the British Isles for over 100 years.

Today, they still work as livestock herders and have become popular and fun family companions and canine agility competitors. Their trainability has also made them successful in police work and search and rescue missions.

## Caretaking Tips

Borders need very vigorous daily exercise. They shine when they have a job, space to run, and an active family life.

They are a breed of high intellect, so training will provide them with much-needed mental stimulation, as well as help focus their strong herding instincts in an appropriate way.

Borders' coats require minimal grooming. They can be brushed two or three times a week, slightly more during shedding season.

# COLLIE

**PHYSICAL CHARACTERISTICS**

The majestic collie (aka rough collie) is one of the most recognizable dog breeds in the world. Medium in stature, they stand 22 to 26 inches tall and weigh 50 to 70 pounds.

Collies boast one of the most beautiful, showy coats of the canine world. The shorter-haired variety, also called the smooth collie, has its own unique charm. Coat colors in both varieties

**DID YOU KNOW?** 🐶

The original Lassie, who appeared in the first movie, *Lassie Come Home* (1943), was a rough collie named Pal. Pal went on to make six more movies and filmed the TV pilot in 1954. Nine more generations of collies also played Lassie.

are sable (brown) and white, tricolor, blue merle (a grayish color), or white.

## PERSONALITY

Collies are a proud, gentle, and sweet-tempered breed. Their fiercely loyal temperament and deep devotion to their families is legendary. Although they will run as hard as they can outside, they are calm and happy to relax with their family inside.

## HISTORY

The ancestors of today's collie were herding dogs in the Scottish Highlands. Queen Victoria put a spotlight on the breed in the 1860s, spurring their popularity among the wealthy upper class.

Collies' popularity in the United States soared to an all-time high in the 1950s, when they became known as the all-American family dog, thanks to a television show called *Lassie*. Today, they continue to rank in the top 50 of the AKC's most popular dog breeds.

### Caretaking Tips

Collies are active dogs who thrive on human companionship and enjoy activities they can share with their people. This is a breed that needs to be engaged because boredom or loneliness can lead to excessive barking. Luckily, collies are bright and easy to train. Training is the perfect activity for them because it combines their love of human companionship and learning new things.

The luxurious double coat of the rough collie requires regular grooming to keep it healthy and free of tangles. They tend to be heavy shedders, especially during shedding seasons, which happen once or twice a year. The smooth collie's coat, although it won't mat, still requires regular grooming.

# GERMAN SHEPHERD

## PHYSICAL CHARACTERISTICS

Large, agile, and hardworking, German shepherds are one of the most versatile, popular, and identifiable breeds in the world today. This breed has a muscular physique with a broad head, large, erect ears, and a bushy tail. They stand 23 to 25 inches tall and weigh between 75 and 95 pounds. Their coat is thick and rough and ranges from shorthaired to longhaired. The most recognizable coat color is black and tan.

## PERSONALITY

German shepherds hold a place in canine royalty for their loyalty, courage, confidence, and high intelligence. They are easygoing and friendly with their families, making them loving companions. They are extremely protective of those they love, also making them excellent watchdogs. Despite

their guarding instincts, it is important to note that well-bred and socialized German shepherds are reserved and not aggressive.

## HISTORY

The German shepherd, or GSD, was developed in Germany in the late 1800s by crossing various herding breeds. Soldiers returning home from World War I first introduced the breed in the United States. By World War II, they were the military breed of choice. They were also the first guide dogs for the blind.

Today, German shepherds can be seen in many lines of work, including service for the blind, search and rescue, and police work. Of course, one of their greatest roles is as treasured companion.

## Caretaking Tips

German shepherds are extremely athletic and intelligent, and they especially enjoy activities they can share with their people. GSDs are easy to train, love to work, and have natural protective instincts that need to be developed in an appropriate way. Early training and socialization are a must with this breed.

Their gorgeous coat needs only moderate grooming. Occasional brushing is sufficient, with additional brushing required during shedding season.

# OLD ENGLISH SHEEPDOG

## PHYSICAL CHARACTERISTICS

Old English sheepdogs are large, solid, athletic dogs hiding under a huge ball of fluff. They range from 21 or 22 inches tall and 60 to 90 pounds. Despite their appearance, they are quite agile and have a distinctive bearlike gait. Their thick, shaggy coat is limited to shades of blue or gray with white patches. Their eyes (when you can see them) are dark brown, blue, or one of each.

## PERSONALITY

Old English sheepdogs are good-natured, intelligent, and kind dogs. They love nothing more than romping around with their family. They are notorious for their sense of humor and clownish antics, making them excellent playmates. They also make

sensible watchdogs known for their loud, ringing bark.

## HISTORY

The modern Old English sheepdog, or OES, originated in England sometime in the early 19th century. They were once used to drive cattle and sheep to market. This is where they developed their "ambling," or strolling, gait. Farmers docked their tails to identify them as drovers' dogs, giving them the nickname Bobtail. (A drover is someone who moves livestock.)

They became prominent in the United States in the late 1800s, when they were shown and bred by wealthy families. Around the 1970s, they were renowned for their comical side and appeared in many films and TV shows. Although they have declined somewhat in popularity over the years, they remain an iconic breed.

**DID YOU KNOW?**

Their coat is highly functional. It is both insulating and waterproof. Additionally, their "woolly" look allowed them to blend in with the flock of sheep they were driving.

### Caretaking Tips

Old English sheepdogs do require a fair amount of exercise and like having tasks to do, whether herding a flock or attending obedience sessions. This is an intelligent breed, rarely forgetting something once they have learned it.

There is no escaping the challenges of grooming this breed. Their coat is labor intensive to maintain and will require frequent trips to a professional groomer.

# PEMBROKE WELSH CORGI

## PHYSICAL CHARACTERISTICS

The smallest of the herding breeds, the Pembroke Welsh corgi is hardy, strong, athletic, and remarkably agile considering its short stature. These dogs are built long and low. At 10 to 12 inches tall and 24 to 28 pounds, this breed packs a great deal of power in its small body.

Unlike the Cardigan Welsh corgi, the Pembroke's tail is closely docked. This, along with their fox-like head and erect ears, make them easily recognizable. The breed's short double coat is waterproof and comes in red, sable, fawn, or black and tan, with or without white markings.

## PERSONALITY

Corgis have become one of the most popular herding breeds due to their lively, affectionate, and friendly nature and unique

proportions. They are bright and sensitive and thrive on being in the center of the action. They make loyal and entertaining companions. Their bold, fearless nature and "big-dog" bark also make them vigilant watchdogs.

## HISTORY

The Pembroke Welsh corgi was developed in Wales in the Pembrokeshire region. The breed was used as an all-around farm dog. They were particularly good with cattle. Pembrokes would nip at the cattle's heels and then duck to avoid their kicks. Pembroke Welsh corgis became widely popular as companion dogs when they became a favorite of Queen Elizabeth II of England. The queen has owned more than 30 corgis during her reign.

**DID YOU KNOW?**

According to Welsh legend, the corgi is an enchanted dog, favored by fairies and elves who would use the dogs to pull their carriages. The markings on the corgi's coat suggest the outline of a saddle and halter.

### Caretaking Tips

Corgis are strong and athletic dogs who need daily physical activity and enjoy having a job to do. Long walks or slow jogs are wonderful for their physical and mental health. Early training and socialization are the keys to a well-adjusted Pembroke Welsh corgi. They do have an independent streak, but overall, they are energetic and willing training partners.

Despite their thick double coat, they only require a quick weekly brushing with just a little extra attention during shedding season.

# Forever Friends

Canines are one of the most diverse species on the planet! With more than 350 breeds worldwide, dogs come in every size, shape, color, and personality. There are no good or bad dogs. Every dog is perfect . . . for someone. The question is, "Is this dog perfect for you?"

The answer can be found through education. I hope this book has started you on your educational journey, answered some of your questions about various breeds, and sparked your interest in learning more about our canine companions. Knowledge of what a breed was developed to do will give you a good idea of how this dog may or may not fit into your life.

Self-knowledge is equally important in finding your forever friend. Who are you? What do you like to do? What are your expectations? Also, what will you bring to this partnership? Will you be able to meet a dog's needs? Knowing and embracing who you are is a key part of the puzzle.

When this knowledge and self-awareness come together, an amazing thing happens—you and your dog are able to form an unbreakable bond based on unconditional love, acceptance, and understanding. That is a gift that lasts a lifetime.

# Resources

**BOOKS**

American Kennel Club. *The Complete Dog Book.* 20th ed. New York: Ballantine Books, 2006.

Brophey, Kim. *Meet Your Dog: The Game-Changing Guide to Understanding Your Dog's Behavior.* San Francisco: Chronicle Books, 2018.

Chin, Lili. *Doggie Language: A Dog Lover's Guide to Understanding Your Best Friend.* London: Summersdale Publishers, 2020.

Van Wye, Mark. *Ultimate Puppy Training for Kids. A Step by Step Guide for Exercises and Tricks.* Emeryville, CA: Rockridge Press, 2020.

**WEBSITES**

www.AKC.org

www.AmericanHumane.org

www.AnimalPlanet.com

www.Dogster.com

www.Rover.com

www.TheBark.com

www.Whole-Dog-Journal.com

## PODCASTS

Boccone, Bud. *Down and Back: Stories from the American Kennel Club Archives,* an American Kennel Club podcast.

> Bud Boccone tells the tales of breeds, dogs, and dog-loving humans who have shaped America over generations.

Colvert, Renee, and Alexis Preston. *Can I Pet Your Dog?,* a Maximum Fun podcast.

> Renee and Alexis discuss dogs they have met, dogs in the news, and dog events.

Hammock, Ashley, and Michael Silver. *About a Dog.*

> A podcast for dog lovers by dog lovers, it looks at dog breeds, their origins, and how they have helped people.

Palika, Liz. *It's A Doggy Dog World,* a Pet Life Radio podcast.

> A podcast all about dogs large, small, and in between; purebred, crossbred, and mixes.

# Index

# About the Author

A lifelong animal lover, **Christine Rohloff Gossinger** ran her own dog-walking and pet-sitting business for 20 years. Her fascination with canine behavior led her to become a certified dog trainer through the FernDog Trainer Academy.

Today, she is a dog trainer with FernDog Training and Tanner's Canine Resort, where her greatest satisfaction and joy is helping pet parents create a positive and lasting bond with their dogs.

She resides in New Jersey with her husband, Mykell, and their fur baby, Bobby, a two-year-old cocker spaniel.

CPSIA information can be obtained
at www.ICGtesting.com
Printed in the USA
JSHW050429190322
23988JS00004B/5